ECHOES OF THE GLEN

OR

MAC-TALLA NAN GLEANN

a

ECHOES OF THE GLEN
OR
MAC-TALLA NAN GLEANN

By

COLIN MACDONALD

THE MORAY PRESS
EDINBURGH *&* **LONDON**

FIRST PUBLISHED 1936

THE MORAY PRESS
126 PRINCES STREET, EDINBURGH
182 HIGH HOLBORN, LONDON, W.C.1

PRINTED IN SCOTLAND
BY THE DUNEDIN PRESS LIMITED, EDINBURGH
AND BOUND BY
WILLIAM HUNTER & SONS, EDINBURGH
FOR
GRANT & MURRAY LIMITED
126 PRINCES STREET, EDINBURGH

CONTENTS

INTRODUCTION

Much of what is contained in this book appeared serially a few years ago in the " Ross-shire Journal " and the " Highland News " and I am indebted to the Editors of these papers for permission to reprint.

I am also much indebted to Mr Alastair MacKillop, Edinburgh, for putting the finishing touches to the Gaelic bits.

The tales and sketches are from actual life as it was lived amongst crofters in a Highland glen some forty to fifty years ago. Personal recollections of that period are particularly interesting because of the striking contrast in type, character and outlook to be found amongst the people who then formed a crofting community.

The railway had just recently extended one of its spreading tentacles to the far north; compulsory education had but recently begun its revolutionizing career: and there was a general widening of the physical and intellectual horizon. So that, at that time there were to be found in the average Highland glen three main classes of people.

First there were the old, who were the last generation in Scotland of the quite illiterate. Generally, they were the descendants of those who had settled in the district following the upheaval caused by the rebellion of 1745. Prior to that event, the clan system with its more or less defined territorial occupation prevailed throughout the Highlands. With the clan system, too, went a minimum in the way of arable cultivation. The easier pastoral system was much more congenial and beef, mutton, venison and fish formed the staple food. When girnals or larders needed replenishing there was always the favourite sport of helping themselves by foray on their more industrious neighbours of the machairs.

But the rebellion and the severe enactments which followed it put an end to the old order. No more was it possible for the Highlanders to supply the family needs by recourse to the sword. In the absence of roads and railways food imports could only come by boat, but in any case, there was no money to pay for them. Necessity is indeed a hard task-master. It forced the ex-clansman to manual labour. He had to turn to the tilling of the soil. But even here there were limitations; for the extent of arable land was meagre. Thus it was that the Highlander was compelled not only to cultivate but to reclaim. For a people so unaccustomed to work they did prodigies in that direction. They trenched the virgin earth, they drained it, they removed stones from it, as huge ramparts of stone dykes still testify; they limed it, they manured it and made it " rich to grow." From 1750 onwards for over a hundred years this work of reclamation went on and it is no exaggeration to state that in 1870 seventy-five per cent. of the whole of the arable land in the Highlands had been laboriously achieved in that way. It should be noted, too, that the arable area in 1870 was considerably in excess of what it is to-day—for much of what the people so industriously reclaimed has been allowed to revert to broom and heather.

These old men and women were purely Gaelic-speaking and many of them did not understand a word of English. In some respects they were undoubtedly ignorant and parochially minded. Their chief concern was with crops and stock and weather and their neighbours' affairs. On the other hand, although unable to read or write they were conversant with interesting old tales and keenly appreciative of such Gaelic poetry and songs as they might hear recited or sung at weddings and other convivial gatherings. Moreover, the very exclusion of those old people from the knowledge that is in books made them entirely dependant for the formation of character and the adjustment of their lives and actions to the world around them on the intelligence, commonsense and charity with which nature had endowed them. Nor was there lack of " the spark of Nature's fire " in many of those old men and women. I can recollect many of them now, who possessed a mien, a dignity and a solidity of character that no mere book-learning can ever bestow.

Then there were the middle-aged, the majority of whom had attended school in their youth for longer or shorter periods; but as attendance was not compulsory, and as the summer and autumn offered opportunities of earning much-needed money at herding and harvest, their school days were usually confined to the winter months. A rudimentary knowledge of the three R's was the extent of their learning at school, and many of them allowed this knowledge, so painfully acquired, to lapse through lack of use. A few, on the other hand, had grasped with greedy clutch this new-found joy. It was a key that could open doors of new worlds to them, and they never ceased to use it. Such were the outstanding men of the district and the acknowledged leaders in all movements calculated to be for the good of the community.

As for the young generation, they, willy nilly went to school from the age of five to fourteen. Encouraged by poor but ambitious parents, and inspired by dreams of their own, the great majority of them sought diligently to acquire such education as would give them a higher market-value in the wider world around them. Equipped with that, and with a good physique in addition to the virtues of decency, frugality and honesty ingrained in their natures by the circumstances of their upbringing, they sought and got employment in many walks of life that drew them away from the Highlands. Year by year the cities claimed them; the colonies; foreign countries; in fact the human drift from the north had set in. And, whether for the ultimate good or ill of those who went, or of the nation as a whole, there can be no doubt whatever that of the various factors which combined to produce the now attenuated Highland population, compulsory education was by far the greatest.

Just as a matter of interest I have measured accurately the extent of drift in the Strath of my youth and it is shown briefly thus: —

	No. of Crofts	Total Population	Population under 20 years
In 1888	57	228	102
In 1936	41	130	33
Decrease	16	98	69

All my life I have been in close contact with crofters. For the first twenty-six years of it it was my privilege to have been one of a crofting community. My oldest and some of my most respected friends are there. Moreover, ours was *the ceilidh* house of the Glen. I can therefore fairly claim to have knowledge of my subject.

It has to be emphasised, though, that the *ceilidh* stories and the conversations as I heard them were in the Gaelic. Even the best English translation or rendering lacks much of the original *blas* (flavour or relish) but that just can't be helped.

There isn't much in the way of dialogue, but where dialogue does occur Highlanders are not made to speak Lowland Scots. That must be disappointing to many, but the truth is, Highlanders do not speak that way. They mostly speak good, if slow and strongly accented King's English.

Moreover, unlike much that I have read concerning the Highlands, what is written here is not culled at second-hand or fanciful, but from personal experience and fact. Of course that may have rendered it less readable, but: —

> 'S fhearr an fhìrinn na'n t-òr,
> 'S cha toil leam a' bhrèug.

Or as it may be rather lamely rendered in the less expressive tongue: —

> Truth transcends treasure;
> The false I despise.

C. MacD.

ECHOES OF THE GLEN
OR
MAC-TALLA NAN GLEANN

CHAPTER I

THE daily round on a croft included—and still includes—a good deal of hard work.

Money was always scarce; so were luxuries; but there was generally a sufficiency of good plain food. This combination of hard work and plain fare—with occasional relaxations—went far towards producing a community that was a poor field for a doctor. One neighbour that I particularly remember whose almost invariable breakfast for over fifty years consisted of brose and milk and oat cake and butter, and whose supper was a repeat of breakfast with porridge substituted for brose, carried on his face the rosy bloom of robust health right through to within a few weeks of his death at eighty-seven, and his only physical troubles were the result of such gastric indiscretions as accompanied the celebration of New Year's Day and such occasions.

Every season as it came round brought its own particular activities. In spring there was the usual bustle associated with ploughing and otherwise preparing the land for the sowing and planting of crops; that was mostly men's work. Summer

A   1

brought with it turnip-thinning and hay-making at which both sexes gave a hand. It also brought peat-cutting which was one of the events of the year. Often there was a neighbourly co-operation in this work; two, three or more families would form a squad that worked together until they had cut peats sufficient for the requirements of all concerned; and anyone who has never had " a day at the peats " has missed a joyous experience. There would, indeed, be exquisitely aching limbs and backs after the first day of that hard work, but these were only subjects for joke and laughter.

The peat-moss in our case lay some four miles distant from the nearest house; the road to it was up a rough cart-track that led, first through the township, then through a shady fir-wood and finally through two miles of heather. The whole squad would be afoot by five o'clock of a sunny summer's morning and ready to start off by six. There would be two or three older folk and maybe a dozen young people in all. There would be baskets packed with oatcakes and scones, fresh butter, home-made jam, hard-boiled eggs and— choicest of all—" speldacks " (a variety of the Finnan Haddock of particularly delicious flavour) for dinner and tea. And the banter and the laughter and the light hearts with which they walked the miles to the moss!

By noon, peats sufficient for some six months' fuel for one house would be cut and spread on the banks to dry; and appetites would be so keen that they would not have quarrelled with much less toothsome fare than was then provided. And Oh! the ecstasy of that meal, spread on an emerald bank by the side of a pirling burn, with the larks pouring out their souls in song in the blue vault overhead!

After dinner the older folk would rest for half an hour while their irrepressible juniors indulged in " soft-peat battles " that are infinitely more ludicrous in their facial " results " than snow-balling. Or, if there was an " innocent " from the south amongst the company the catch of *leum nan tri fòidean* (the three peat jump) would be tried out. For this practical joke—highly diverting to the onlookers and even laughed at by the victim—a spot was chosen at the edge of a deep peat hag which contained a pool of black, peaty water. Those in the know would start a competition in " standing " long-jump; they jumped from the edge of the hag, and landed on the lower level across the pool. When the competition got very keen an expert would suggest that much longer jumps could be achieved if the start was made from a slightly higher level. To demonstrate his theory he would lay three hard peats one above the other on the heather close to the edge of the hag and parallel to it. He then stood on top of the peats and jumped. But he had to be very careful to spring almost vertically so as not to disturb the peats by the backward pressure of the toes; he just managed to clear the pool as a rule

—sometimes he did not, and I have seen the biter bit! But, assuming no such initial catastrophe, the " innocent " was allowed a try. He—or she—never suspecting a trap, stood on the peats and jumped in the ordinary way—with disastrous results! The backward pressure of the toes at the moment of taking the spring caused the piled peats to tumble backwards and the athlete to take an involuntary header into the black mess below!

Sleep came without rocking that night; but the muscular pains and aches of next morning were in a class by themselves! However, another hard day at the peats was an effective, if heroic, remedy.

Scarcely any coal was used, and the annual fuel requirement of the township ran to 2,500 loads of peat. As the years went by the difficulty of getting squads increased. Coal had to be resorted to and by 1925 had so completely ousted the old fuel that in that year not one load of peats was burned in the whole of the Strath.

CHAPTER II

HARVEST was the busiest and most anxious season
of the year, yet it had a cheery atmosphere too.
There was a full family muster at the work which
was of such vital importance to all; everyone from
eight to eighty gave a hand. On the larger farms
in the valley reaping machines were in use. " Self-
delivery " reapers were at that time just coming
in, and their revolving wings, besides performing
the work of the second man, lent an added appearance of activity to the field. But—with the
exception of one proud possessor of an antiquated
" tilter "—all the crofters cut their crop with the
scythe. The day of the heuk had just passed.

The scythe gang consisted of three people; the
" scyther " who cut the crop with such rhythmic
sweeps of his awkward looking implement and laid
it in an orderly row by his left side; the " lifter "
(usually a woman) who gathered the crop into
sheaf-size and laid it on bands deftly made by
herself from a small handful of straightened
straws; and lastly, the " binder-and-stooker "

5

(either sex) who tied the sheaves and stooked them.

Given favourable conditions—a standing crop, a dry day and a gentle breeze—the gang would finish an acre in a day of ten hours. Sometimes, when neighbours joined forces at harvest as they did at peat-cutting and there might be as many as six gangs working together, the harvest field presented an animated scene as the six scythes, side by side, but each one on the right, back a yard from the one on the left, bit their way into the standing crop with a rhythm and timing that resembled the measures of a good-going song.

The state of the weather at harvest, was, of course, the great factor which determined the time necessary for the attainment of that coveted last-cut handful of the year's crop, the *Maighdeann Bhuana*, which was duly decorated with gaily-coloured ribbons and hung on the kitchen wall till New Year's morning when it was presented to the old mare in a spirit of mixed fun and solemnity.

In all but exceptional years the middle of October saw the crop all under broom thatch and *sioman* (straw rope). And then what romping fun we youngsters used to have running round the stacks playing *Cluich-nan-cruach* (the fun of the stacks) . . . ! It was keenly exciting, this stalking and chasing each other round the new-made stacks by the light of *Gealach bhuidhe Feill-Mhicheil* (the yellow moon of Michaelmas). The fun was liable to be spoilt, though, by the older lads and lassies retiring to dark corners for some quiet "coortin" (*suiridhe*)—much to the disgust of the wee ones—until they grew older themselves!

A few loads of sheaves were destined never to go into a stack. They were put straight into the barn for early threshing. This was for the double purpose of providing a straw supper (*Muillean Fodair*) for the beasts whose pastures were now rather bare, and the household with the first oatmeal of the season. I suppose the beasts will still require to get their supper, but I'm thinking there is not the same demand for the *Min-Chorca* that used to taste so good!

After harvest there was a rush to get the potatoes lifted before Hallowe'en, for it was rather a discreditable mark to have potatoes still unlifted on the first of November. By this time, too, the first oatmeal of that year's crop would be in the girnal and there was a general feeling of security against the coming winter.

Winter was ushered in by the celebration of Hallowe'en; a festival of joyous adventure for the youths who formed raiding bands that "stole" neighbours' carts and ploughs and swingle-trees, and, by a process of interchanging wheels and axles, etc., contrived to give a few puzzling days to the owners. Anything in the nature of malicious mischief was debarred by the etiquette of the fun, but those few crofters who were foolish enough to resent this somewhat inconveniencing but harmless youthful frolic might rest assured of added and special attention when next Hallowe'en came round. And we were specially fortunate when two of our principal oppressors happened to be at variance with each other and not on speaking terms. That was a heaven-sent opportunity of achieving an amazing mix-up of carts and wheels and axles and ploughs and socks and swingle-trees which it took the hostile owners weeks to unravel; indeed sometimes the riddle could only be solved by the helpful intervention of one of the original but unsuspected perpetrators!

On the other hand, neighbours who didn't resent our frolics and who left their ploughs and carts in the open, were seldom molested. There was no fun, for instance, in running off with anything belonging to *Uilleam Ruairidh,* for *Uilleam* left his gear unchained and unprotected and would never say an angry word if we went off with the lot.

So, instead of " stealing " *Uilleam's* gear, fantastically dressed and with blackened faces, we would pay a friendly call, announcing our arrival with a fusillade of turnips on the door.

Uilleam's attitude was not the result of calculating diplomacy; he was a kindly old man, living all by himself—and his dog Sharpy—genuinely fond of young folks and with a delightfully sympathetic understanding of their ways. He could read fortunes, too, in the white of an egg—a much more reliable medium than mere cards or tea-cups—and many a merry winter evening did the lads and

lassies spend in *Uilleam's* cheery kitchen as he
" saw " their various fortunes in the bubbles of
the *Gealagan*.

One morning after Hallowe'en *Eilidh Dhonn's*
chimney would not draw for the reason that
Maoilean's washing-pot had been placed upside-
down on the lum. Two of us climbed on to the
roof and removed the obstruction. We had the
grace to feel a little guilty on receiving much
praise and a handful of " lozengers " from dear
old *Eilidh*—for well we knew how the pot had got
there!

Then there was the day the *Taillear Fada* and
his wife slept in " *An latha rinn sinn moch-eirigh* "
(" The day we did the early rising ")—as himself
used facetiously to refer to the incident.

It took a lot of doing, but we did manage without being discovered to plug up the windows and
round the *Taillear's* door with a plaster of soft
peat so that not a *dideag* (peep) of light could
enter the house. As the *Taillear* never possessed
a clock but regulated his rising and retiring by
the light of the sun, the ruse succeeded beyond
our brightest expectations. It was the persistent
ranail of the beasts in the byre that at last impelled
the *Taillear* to open the door—and there, to his
astonishment, was the sun at twelve o'clock!

CHAPTER III

As winter progressed towards the shortest days of the year, field work lessened, and there was opportunity for attending to the hundred and one things that needed repair or renewal. Leather harness needed sewing; belts required to be mended; hoes and rakes needed new teeth or handles; corn riddles required new bottoms or frames; turnip and potato-baskets made of wild willow were repaired or made anew; the family boots had to be patched and soled—in fact there was scarcely a limit to the number of such indoor and necessary occupations on a well-managed croft.

Yet winter was not all devoted to work, and there was a surprising number of ways in which the long winter evenings could be made to pass pleasantly.

Despite the frown with which the majority of clergymen of that day regarded dancing, youth would out, and so would dancing. One winter, when there had grown up in the Glen a young generation who knew no dancing because of the ecclesiastical opposition which had for several years suppressed tentative efforts at organising a dancing class, a few lads set the ministerial wrath at defiance. They engaged a dancing-master, and, as there was no suitable hall available for their purpose, they arranged with an elderly crofter of youthful daring for the use of an old thatched barn. The barn had only an earthen floor and its roof showed generous patches of sky; but our heroes clubbed together and between them raised funds and labour sufficient to repair the roof and put in a wooden floor. That was a memorable winter; practically every young person in the place joined the class—and in those days we *danced*.

To me those modern dances introduced from the U.S.A. are an anaemic exhibition. There is nothing to them at all. You just go slithering your feet along the floor in any old way you choose. There does not appear to be any definite relationship of step to music. The main effort is in the direction of avoiding effort; and, if you please, after but a few minutes of this wildly unexciting stuff the musicians very considerately stop to give the poor things a rest. But the latter clap their hands in dull unison to signify their wish to carry on a little longer. So the music and the inanity start off again!

But where are the dances of forty years ago? Quadrilles and Lancers with their stately grace and timing? The Highland Schottische that in its first part was the epitome of accurate step-control, and in its second stage demanded such chivalrous skill in steering clear of calamity in the joyous swinging swirl? Petronella? How your top couple

used to race " down the middle," warm hand in
hand, and then " back again and waltz round."
You could be danced properly to one tune only;
but that tune was an inspiration, and it was
unworthy of us to dub it as we did, " The Cat took
the Measles and she died, poor thing " !

And the romp of Rory O'More!—and the
quaint deferential gallantries in Sir Roger de
Coverley—better known as the Haymakers' Jig
. . . !

Polka!   Pas-de-quatre!   Circassian Circle!
Flowers of Edinburgh!   These are some of the
names that we then responded to so heartily, and
that now recall our fondest memories.

But high above them all, in actuality and retrospect, stood and stands the Scotch Reel and Reel
o' Tulloch. For that was more than a mere dance:
it was a medium for expression of national and
individual character. When the master of cere-
monies announced the magic name the floor filled
in a flash, and from the initial sweeping courtesy
to the glorious final flourish it was an inspired
poem of physical activity and spiritual satiety. O,
Jimac-o-Davie!—that used to stamp out " time "
with your tackety toes (for a real reel pumps are a
futility) so that you inspired Georgie's elbow to
magic with his fiddle—which in turn inspired you
to higher, and still higher abandon of heel and
hand and hoochs that rose in grand crescendo to
the culminating crash. . . .   What would you say
to the so-called dances of to-day?   To the Fox-Trot,

the One-step and the Two-step with their slithering feet and timeless, tuneless pusillanimity? I can hear your scornful " *Air falbh leo! Cha'n fhiach iad!* "—(" Away with them! They are worthless! ")

There was a never-to-be-forgotten grand finale in the shape of a ball in the village hall—in close proximity to the Manse! Whatever credit fell to be ascribed to the clergy of those days would certainly not include an item for *intentionally* adding brightness and happiness to the lives of their parishioners.

CHAPTER IV

VERY little notice was taken of Christmas Day and
it was not until the "eighties" that the first of
January began to be celebrated in our circle as
New Year's Day, and even in those houses where
the new fashion was adopted there was a celebration on Old New Year's Day too. Many families
did not take to the new fashion—in their own
homes—for twenty or thirty years after that.
Indeed, there is a remnant of respect for Old New
Year's Day in the shape of a neighbourly dram
still to be met with on the east end of the Strath.
For many years both fashions were observed in one
house or another, with the result that there was a
more or less continuous celebration from the night
of 31st December till the 13th January. However, whisky cost only 2/3 per bottle—"Special"
2/6—and it was whisky! There would be first-
footing and feasting and singing and dancing to
surfeit.

But the event of New Year's Day itself was the
game of shinty.

There was no limit to the number which might
form a team. Everyone was enlisted on one side

or another and it was not uncommon to see in the game men of seventy and boys of seven. There might not be much method or combination in the play of a team, but there were great individual players who could do miracles to the *cnag* (ball) with the aid of a home-made *caman* which was treasured for years for this annual outing.

One game I remember was captained on the one side by a man of sixty years of age and the other by a sixty-two year old. They had been opposing captains for years and the closest of friends all their lives. Both were over six feet and as lean as a lath. They met on the field of play about eleven o'clock, each carrying his trusty home-made *caman*. Of course, several drams had already been downed and many *slainte mhaths* and *Bliadhna-mhathùrs* (Good-healths and Good-New-Years) exchanged.

The method of selecting sides is interesting. The two captains stood facing each other. *Dònull* held his *caman* by the middle and threw it vertically towards *Uilleam* who caught it where he could with one hand. Then each in turn took a hand-over-hand grip of the *caman* towards the top. The last to get a grip at the top and be able, with that grip, to swing the *caman* three times round his head had first call on the crowd for his side. They then called in turn till everybody was enrolled. Then off went jackets—which were piled to form " hail-posts " at either end of the field, and then. . . . !

Modern hockey players consider modern shinty

a wild and dangerous game. I wonder what they would think of the shinty served up by the grand-fathers! Even on a New Year's Day " friendly " play would be wild enough, but should it be a real match between rival parishes, then indeed it was no field for falterers.

Foul?—There was none. No quarter given or asked.

" *Cluich suas! Sid thu Iain! Buail a' Bhug . . !* " —(I'm not translating that one).

Skin and hair went flying in real style. A bloody face or limb was a mark of honour, and by the end of two hours' fierce encounter few indeed were scathless. At the New Year friendly generous " revivers " were resorted to frequently during the match, but so hard was the game that every man was as sober as a judge by one o'clock, and partook of an amazing meal of broth and beef and potatoes which the good-wife of the house had prepared in three large washing-pots.

CHAPTER V

A School for Orators.

OUR Strath was rather singular in that, since the early seventies it had a properly constituted and well-conducted Debating Society which met two or three evenings each week from October to April. For the first twenty years the Society had rather a precarious existence. It had plenty spiritual heat but no material home. One winter it met in the smiddy. For some years an old thatched barn was its temple. Again, a granary housed it for a while; and one winter, when the local station-master was its president, the Highland Railway waiting-room sheltered its enthusiastic members. Moreover, at the end of that session the proceeds of a collection were applied to purchasing paraffin in substitution of the Company's paraffin consumed throughout the winter. There seemed to be a kindlier contact between railway officials and the public in those days than is possible with the present soul-less combine—and no whit less honesty.

Later—as recent as thirty-nine years ago—the Society became sufficiently strong and enthusiastic to erect a small hall as its permanent headquarters.

There followed a period of much activity and progress; then decay; and now, for over twenty years, not a vestige of the old Debating Society—only the little hall—sadly forsaken—but for its ghosts. . . .

In addition to the debates there were magazine-nights, hat-nights, draughts, etc. A youth was eligible for membership on attaining the age of fifteen, and no member of parliament ever took his first seat with keener pride and apprehension than did our initiates on their first night.

A young member was not compelled by rule to speak other than very briefly during his first session, but in subsequent years it was obligatory on everyone to take a responsible part in debate. There were some, of course, who never became fluent or interesting speakers, but there were several who did, and who could express their well considered opinions in concise, consecutive form and cool collected manner that stood them in good stead in future years in various walks of life.

CHAPTER VI

The Ceilidh—Patronymics—The Land League.

But the pastime par excellence of the winter months was the *ceilidh*. It seems incredible that nearly fifty years can have elapsed since those well-remembered *ceilidh* evenings with their kindly gossip and stories of events and characters of long ago.

Of all words and institutions, this of *ceilidh* is surely now the most misrepresented and abused! It never gives me real pleasure to say anything nasty of anybody, but I cannot help thinking that those Highland Associations of the South which in recent years have been foisting on their members and the general public those so-called *ceilidhs* of theirs have much to answer for.

A *ceilidh* where you have to pay to get in!—in a hall!—with a platform!—and a chairman!— in a boiled shirt!—and the folks all dressed up!— and a programme!—and set speeches!—and everyone so mincingly polite with the mimmery of a formal concert! *Mo Naire! Mo Naire!* Call it a gathering. Call it a concert. Call it a Highland Concert if you will: but do not call it a *ceilidh*.

A *ceilidh* was not a fore-ordered thing: it was a

natural growth. Only round a kitchen peat fire could it flourish. Nobody was bidden. Anybody came. There was absolute social equality. The sartorial peak never rose beyond a clean collar and brushed whiskers. The talk just came— easily—naturally. One topic led to another. Each was free to talk or listen. Although, naturally, some excelled, never was the *ceilidh* a " show-off " place for the individual. There was utter camaraderie, utter " off-guard." There was an easy friendly understanding atmosphere about the *ceilidh* that I have never quite met in any other kind of gathering—and when they rose to go, " *cabhag air do thilleadh* " (hasten your return) from *Bean an tighe* (the House-wife) adequately expressed everybody's sentiments.

Perhaps nothing can so emphasise the equality that pervaded the *ceilidh*—and throughout the crofting community for that matter—as their mode of addressing each other. There was no " mister " at all. One man to another was just *Dònull* or *Ruairidh* or *Alasdair* or whatever his Christian name was. Two of the same name were distinguished from each other by some special qualification, as *Mor* (big) or *Beag* (little), or it might be by the addition of his father's or grandfather's Christian name or craft. An art or craft, even if not practised in the family for generations might still be the distinguishing patronymic. Often, indeed, the legal name of a person was practically forgotten. There were more than a dozen old people in the Strath whose proper names I never knew until curiosity set me inquiring—and then, some of those I asked weren't too sure!

A married woman, whether widow or wife, was addressed as the wife of her husband. If her husband's name was—or had been—*Dònull,* she was addressed as *" Bean Dhònuill "*—with a tendency to add the distinguishing patronymic of her man.

Even neighbouring children adopted this mode of address towards their elders—and never with disrespect. Unmarried women were invariably known by their Christian names. To be addressed as " Miss " was a great joke.

It was when the big snow-storms came that real good *ceilidhs* were possible, because then no outside work could be done and responsibilities were limited to the feeding of the beasts and barnwork. Then when night came—often, it seems now, with a bright moon shining over a world of white, but at intervals darkened by wild showers of drifting snow—one after another of the neighbours would drop in. Inside there was a blazing peat fire that sent its welcome warmth to every corner of the kitchen. The bairns were gathered round a table busy at lessons. The good-man had pulled in the old arm-chair to the fire-side and adjusted his spectacles—bought from a pedlar for one-and-sixpence and a fill of tobacco, and, by the simple test of efficiency equal to any modern lenses costing two guineas—preparatory to having a preliminary glance at the contents of one of the local news-papers. It might be "The Ross-shire Journal" (still flourishing), at that time execrated by all crofters for its Tory views on the land question, but bought weekly because of the necessity of finding out the moves of the enemy. Or it might be that staunch supporter (now defunct) of the land agitation, the "Invergordon Times." The good-wife, whose amazing variety and volume of work went on from early morning till late at night, and whose robust health and intense interests made her life a real joy compared to the drab exis-tence of the working man's wife in the city, would probably be knitting or sewing or darning.

There was no formal knocking at doors in those days, and the first indication of an arrival for the *ceilidh* was the sound of thumping and stamping of feet outside, and finally of slapping with a broom or heather besom to remove the snow from boots and leggings. Then a loud hail: "*Cò tha stigh?*" (Who is within). "That will be Dònull; let him in," the good-man would say to one of the bairns. Someone ran to open the door and to smile a welcome.

In the course of the next hour half a dozen others—and sometimes more than twice that num-ber—would arrive. A more homogeneous lot it would be difficult to imagine; yet they were a study in contrasts. Nearly every man was a rank individualist and only subscribed to another's opinion if, after critical discussion and mature consideration he felt he was justified in doing so.

At that period there was a strong move on the part of crofters throughout the Highlands to obtain statutory fair rents, security of tenure and the right to compensation for permanent improvements effected on their holdings. Branches of the Land League had been formed in nearly every parish, and feeling between crofters and estate factors ran pretty high. I shall not discuss here the merits or otherwise of the case on either side, but no one who witnessed the *ceilidh* on an evening when the activities of the Land League were under discussion can ever forget the scene. Seated in his arm chair by the side of the fire with the eyes and ears of the whole *ceilidh* circle giving him rapt attention, the good-man would read what one of the papers had to say about the matter in its leading article, or what others' views were as expressed in " Letters from Correspondents." A short paragraph would be read, then the spectacles would be removed, and, changing to the Gaelic, the reader would make the point crystal clear to his audience in their mother tongue. When the point was thoroughly taken by all, the process would be repeated, again and again, until the end of the article was reached, and then everyone joined in general discussion. It was indeed an impressive scene.

CHAPTER VII

DONULL was one of the outstanding men of the *ceilidh*. He would come in stroking and blowing the snow from his red beard. He was a low-set sturdily built man, the embodiment of health and vigour and the kindliest of neighbours—although very critical of those who slept long of mornings! He himself was up at five a.m. summer and winter. His chimney put up the first smoke in the parish. He could tell to a minute when the other smokes went up, and after many years of close observation of the point he had by this guage arrived at a rough estimate of the relative worthiness of every family in the place. He had practically no book-learning, but he had a wonderful knowledge of Gaelic songs and sayings; and for native intelligence, wit and humour, I have seldom met his superior. Dònull had a rare knack of gathering news and as he was a born *raconteur* his way of retailing it was a lesson in elocution. Moreover, he had a retentive memory and could quote from such Gaelic bards as Duncan Bàn, Rob Donn and Ross of Gairloch with unerring aptitude to the

24

tale in hand. He was the only farmer in a district of crofters but he entertained no snobbish views of social superiority on that account and was always " one of ourselves." Old and young welcomed Dònull to the *ceilidh* for his presence assured them of an interesting and merry evening.

We bairns just loved to lure Dònull on to telling the story of

THE CAILEAG BHEAG BHAN

or

THE LITTLE FAIR-HAIRED LASSIE

The *Caileag Bheag* was really an ancestor of Dònull's own, and the story came down to him from his mother who had got it from her grandfather:

Away back in the distant past the people of Dònull's clan were at strong enmity with a clan who lived three days' journey away. Fights and forays between them were of frequent occurrence. One day didn't the *Caileag Bheag Bhàn*—then only two years of age and the darling of the district —go amissing. High and low they searched for her; by the burn-side, in the heather, in the woods. But never a trace of their darling could they find, and sore, sore were their hearts for many a long day.

Eighteen years later a young man of Dònull's clan was returning from the wars in Holland. For short cut he chanced going through the old enemy territory. But he had to go warily for, if discovered, he might never reach home.

He was stealthily winding his way up a burnside where the hazel bushes, open spaces and sparkling fern-fringed pools were transformed by the afternoon sun into a veritable fairy-land. Suddenly Tormaid Og stood spell-bound! Across the clearing by the side of a pool, clad in dress of green bracken and with a garland of wild flowers in her hair, stood the most beautiful *Caileag* he had ever seen! But she was no immortal.

Utterly unconscious of his near presence the *Caileag* began to sing in a voice—oh! so sweet and tuneful! And, to Tormaid's amazement, the song was a croon of his own clan!

Fearful lest he should frighten away so lovely a creature Tormaid decided on a ruse. When she came to the end of a verse in which the mother asked the little one—now on the point of sleep— what had she to be afraid of—for would not the big brothers of the clan keep her safe, Tormaid remembered the response that came from the big brother and this he sang in low melodious voice. The response came so naturally that at first the *Caileag Bheag* did not seem to realise that it was an actual human being who made it. But before she could take alarm Tormaid Og said: —

" Fear not, *mo chaileag Bheag Bhàn.* A friend

is near you. Nay, not merely a friend but a kinsman. For surely those features and tresses of yours belong not here but to my clan. And the croon? " said he, " Where learned you the croon that is ours? "

Assured by the friendliness in his voice the *Caileag* explained that she had thought she belonged to the local clan and that they were all so good and kind to her; but that of late she had been dissatisfied and a yearning for, she knew not what, had come over her. As for the croon, she did not know where it came from. It and the music of it just " swam into her heart " one day.

But Tormaid pointed out that it must be the unconscious recollection that came to her of what her mother used to sing her to sleep with as a child.

Events followed joyfully after that. The *Caileag Bheag Bhàn* knew Tormaid Og was speaking truth and straightway went home with him to her own people. Great was the rejoicing amongst young and old.

For a time there was fear of a raid by the ancient enemy; but it soon transpired that the latter were as fond of the *Caileag Bheag Bhàn* as were her own people; and, as the great desire of both sides was for her happiness they agreed to enter a friendly compact—and so ended the old enmity for ever.

Of another type entirely was Dònull's story of

UISDEAN MOR AND MAIRI BHOIDHEACH

or

BIG HUGH AND BONNIE MAIRI

Uisdean was a strapping lad of twenty-five and foreman on one of the big farms in the valley.

Mairi was twenty-two and dairymaid at the same place. She lived with her widowed mother in a cottage half a mile from the farm and was just as nice and bonnie a lassie as you could meet on a day's journey.

For five years Uisdean had been courting Mairi but for some reason or another had never come to the scratch. It began to look as if he might prolong the courting stage indefinitely. Needless to say, this prospect did not please Mairi. The *Maighstir* (Master), too, an observant, kindly old man with whom Mairi was a great favourite, had taken stock of what was going on and was getting impatient at Uisdean's dilly-dallying.

Every term day the *Maighstir* would say to Mairi, " I suppose I will be losing you, *'Mhairi 'ghalad,* by the end of the next term? " But ever it was the same doubtful reply.

Then one evening the *maighstir* and Mairi put their *comhairle cuideachd* (consulted together) and things began to happen next morning.

It was the day of the Muir-of-Ord Market. By five in the morning the maighstir was ready for off, grey pony and *breacan* (plaid) all complete. Then of a sudden he remembered! He shouted for Uisdean.

" Uisdean," said he, " run as fast as your legs will take you to Mairi's house and ask her if she will do me the favour of lending me a hundred pounds till to-morrow. I need the money for the Muir to-day and I forgot that this was a bank holiday! "

Uisdean opened wide his eyes and stared. Then he scratched his head and concluded that the maighstir had gone insane! But anyway, the maighstir was insistent.

" Off you go! " said he in well simulated wrath, " and don't stand there like a choking hen! "

And to humour the madman Uisdean ran off on his fool's errand.

Mairi was just leaving home for the day's work when Uisdean arrived.

" It's a fine morning, Uisdean," Mairi greeted him with a becoming flush. " But what is all the hurry? Is anything wrong at the farm? "

" Wrong," exclaimed Uisdean. " If the maighstir hasn't gone off his head! "

" Indeed! indeed! " said Mairi, " It's myself that is sorry! And how has it taken him? "

" Taken him! " said Uisdean, " hasn't he sent me here like a fool to ask if you will lend him a hundred pounds for the Muir-of-Ord to-day! "

" Ach! and is that all? " retorted Mairi, apparently greatly relieved, " And why should he be

off his head to ask that? Indeed it is myself that
will lend him the money and welcome. Come
you in for a minute till I get it."

Uisdean was dumfounded but followed Mairi
in amazement into the cottage. Mairi went to
her *ciste* (trunk), took out a fat roll of £1 notes
and deliberately counted out a hundred of them.
Then said she to the now nearly petrified Uisdean.

" Are you sure it was only a hundred he wanted
because he is welcome to more? "

Uisdean was just able to assure her that it was
a hundred pounds the maighstir had mentioned.

" Off with you, then! " urged Mairi, " and don't
let the decent man be late for the market! "

Uisdean and Mairi were married at the next
Martinmas term, and they lived happily to a very
old age. I happen to know and esteem their descendants this very day.

Mairi always kept ten £1 notes rolled over a wad
of newspaper locked away in her *ciste*. But she
wisely never told Uisdean that that was the
maighstir's wedding present, or that these and the
hundred pounds she " loaned " on that memorable
morning had been given her by the maighstir the
night before for that very purpose—and to bring
a laggard lover to the point!

CHAPTER VIII

Seumas the Philosopher—Calum : a close shave—Sian : the
 protective charm.

ANOTHER outstanding character was *Seumas*. He
was comparatively well educated and had a small
but select library. He got two or three weekly
papers and one monthly magazine—Stead's
" Review of Reviews "—and sometimes he had
American and other foreign papers and periodicals
sent to him from friends abroad. Seumas did not
come often to the *ceilidh,* but when he did come
mere gossip was taboo for that evening. Stories
of pioneer life in Canada or Australia and political
or ethical dissertations were his sort of contribution
and I can yet see the eager interest of the less
well-informed as they listened to his graphic dis-
course. Seumas was at once the best and the worst
crofter in the district. He always had good crops
and stock and was held in great respect by his
neighbours, but accomplishments in which other
men took supreme pride—for instance, a straight
furrow or a well-built stack—were matters of utter
indifference to him. I have seen him nearing a
" finish " in his lea ploughing with the unploughed
rig yards wide at one end and run to nothing at
the other, and " a straight like a corkscrew." When

I mildly twitted him on the point he laughed unconcernedly, and told me that it was only when I mentioned the matter he realised he *was* ploughing; he had spent the whole forenoon just following the horses and absently turning over the ground, but his thoughts had been occupied with some poem of Burns, the run of which he had been trying to get right!

" But," said he, " although the furrows are crooked the oats will grow just as well as if they were straight; " and so they did, for he always used the best of seed and kept his land in a high state of fertility.

On another occasion I was giving him a hand with the leading-in of the harvest; he was building the stack and I was forking on. He kept up an interesting conversation all the time and I had to warn him repeatedly that the stack was going agee. He did try to rectify matters, but usually overdid it until, when nearly finished the stack had assumed rather a weird shape, but the builder's concern was with something in Russia. Just as the last of the standing sheaves were being fitted in at the top the whole structure came toppling to earth—with the architect half-buried in the ruins! To most stackers such a happening would have seemed a calamity but my philosophic friend merely grasped an armful of sheaves, started to build again on a new foundation, and proceeded with the tale of Siberia!

CALUM—A CLOSE SHAVE

Calum came from the west end of the Strath. He was an old soldier and had been with the Seaforths in Egypt at the battle of Tel-el-Kebir. His stories of personal encounters and blood and battles were of a kind that made Buffalo Bill's exploits seem comparatively anaemic. How we revelled in Calum's stories!—in the telling of which I am convinced he never sacrificed colour and effect for veracity. But one could not doubt the truth of that time when the great big Dervish with a ferocious face ran at Calum with the very obvious intention of plunging a long-hefted spear through his entrails; or of how Calum, partly in terror and partly because his Highland blood was up, side-stepped smartly—he always emphasised the celerity of that particular side-step—and turned the tables by plunging his bayonet—a grand "third point with the lunge"—right into his assailant's diaphragm until the point came out at the back! I can still hear the squelch with which that son of Pharaoh fell in his tracks. But not before his spear (deviated somewhat from its true aim by the accident to its owner) had pierced the side of Calum's body just outside the ribs. The wound soon healed up, but the ceilidh puzzle was: how did Calum come to be wounded at all? For had not his old neighbour, *Mairi Mhor*, put the *sian* on him before he went away to the war? —the *sian* which was a sure shield against all

C

injury by enemy missiles? However, it was comforting to reflect that that one small wound was the only evidence of its inefficacy; and, indeed, taking into consideration the size and ferocity of this particular Dervish, was not the slight wound rather a proof of its *efficacy*?

CHAPTER IX

An Taillear Fada and his "Alteration."

AND who that ever saw—and heard—the *Taillear Fada* (The Long Tailor) could ever forget him? The *Taillear* was actually six feet six inches in height but he was so thin—we used to say we would thread him through a darning needle— that he gave the impression of being over seven feet at least. His voice was something unique: it had only one tone and volume and these were of such stentorian character that they would make the best efforts of a Sergeant-Major on parade seem feeble. When, therefore, as frequently happened, the *Taillear* and his wife had a difference of opinion over some domestic detail, and when the argument was conducted—as it usually was—out-of-doors, all the neighbours within a mile radius could listen-in with the greatest of ease and be thoroughly informed as to the *Taillear's* opinion of his consort. Her retorts might be inaudible to the listeners but judging from the ire they seemed to arouse in her husband they must have been very much to the point. As I grew older and got to know this strange couple intimately I was surprised to find that they got on

35

very well together and were really quite fond of each other. I could only conclude, therefore, that those wordy wars were merely a sort of training for " keeping their hand in " at the art of crushing retort—an accomplishment in which both were ever expert.

When the *Taillear Fada* came to the ceilidh, the others generally manoeuvred him into telling the story of that time he went all the way to Edinburgh Hospital for the " alteration " (operation) to his leg. He rode part of the way on " Rory," a very small horse for such a long-legged man. One of Rory's successors that I remember was also small, and when his master bestrode him the long legs just reached the ground; and when the rider wanted to dismount he did so by the simple process of standing on his toes and commanding Rory to " go on "—which Rory did—leaving his master standing on mother-earth behind him.

I will not tell here of the adventures on the journey south, but the experience in hospital must be touched on. The first problem was an adequate bed; the one that had been prepared for him was too short. When that was ultimately overcome there was trouble about the sheets: the patient complained that they were cold and " slippery." But the matron was firm, and sleep in sheets he had to—for the first and last time in his life. Then when the doctor came to see the patient and turned down the bed-clothes for the purpose of examining the leg he gazed in astonishment and exclaimed,

"Good Lord! What a length!" Shortly afterwards that doctor went out and brought in another
who immediately on viewing the *Taillear* exclaimed, "My God! What a length!" And yet
a third doctor was brought in and his first remark
was "Good Lord! What a length of a man!"
These outspoken comments on his person annoyed
our friend, but he restrained his anger and said
not a word (" *Cha dubhairt mi guth!* ") But when,
on the morning of the "Alteration" he was put
into a waggon and wheeled through to the operat-
ing theatre where there were several "stoodants,"
and when the latter on seeing our hero whispered
practically in chorus, "Good Lord! what a length
of a man!" it was too much for the *Taillear,* who
raised his head and addressed them firmly—and
do not forget the voice—"Com, com, you there!
What you are going to do, do it, and never mind
your 'what a man!'—and non of your cloryforum
for me neither!" It was in the early days of
chloroform and it had been suggested to the patient
that some of the new drug should be administered
to ease the pain. But the patient would have none
of it, and the bone was exposed and scraped, and
the only indication of pain on the part of the
Taillear was that he chewed a bit off the sheet—
and he didn't like sheets anyway!

CHAPTER X

ALASTAIR was a general favourite throughout the neighbourhood. He seldom missed a ceilidh, but his usual role there was that of appreciative listener. His philosophy seemed to have led him to the conclusion that it wasn't worth while holding on to any point of view so strongly as to involve one in a quarrel or heated argument. It is true that occasionally—perhaps twice in the course of a year; once when the stirks were sold and again on the rent day—when a certain degree of victory over the ills of life had been attained, anyone who put any proposition to this usually complaisant man would find that he had caught a Tartar. For, under the inspiring influence of a few hours in the village inn Alastair would argue any point with anybody! Not in a nasty spirit, but in a jovial, loquacious, and delightfully witty manner so utterly unlike his usual quiescence that he would hold the stage for that evening.

Telling of Alastair brings his neighbour, Ranald, to the memory. Ranald's prestige in the ceilidh circle lay in the fact that he had been in the Crimean War. This old campaigner had lain with

38

the British Army for months outside Sebastopol.
The siege was a long, drawn-out affair, and a certain degree of friendship grew up between the
soldiers on either side, but more particularly
between the opposing sentries, a number of whom
had got to recognise each other and " conversed "
by signs and actions in quite a friendly way.

But there was one highly unpopular black-
bearded " Rooshian " who was given to express
his contempt for the British by gestures which have
a common meaning in all languages. This man,
as he did sentry-go on top of the city wall had
often roused the ire of the British sentry opposite
by his insulting " language," and there had been
many threats of reprisal; but there was a strict
order that no shot was to be fired except for the
purpose of giving the alarm of some serious move-
ment on the part of the enemy. The insults,
therefore, went unavenged until one day, when
Ranald was doing sentry-go, the " linguist " sur-
passed his previous efforts by raucously clearing
his throat and expectorating in Ranald's direction;
then he put his thumb to his nose with fingers
outspread, and finally—a new " phrase "—he
turned his back and smote with his hand that part
of the anatomy which is normally sat on. This
enraged the Highlander who shook his fist and
pointed to his rifle to indicate that if the insult
was repeated he would shoot. The Russian must
have reckoned that this was just an idle threat
because he proceeded to repeat the insult down to

the last detail; at which moment Ranald snatched up his rifle, took hurried aim, and fired. He was a noted shot, and on this occasion proved up to his best standard, for he registered a bull's eye on the offending hand and its tender underlying support—to the extreme discomfiture of the guardian of the city, who gave a loud yell, disappeared round a corner of the ramparts, and was never again seen on that section of the wall.

But the report of the shot roused the whole British Army; buglers sounded the " stand-to " and there was general commotion. Ranald realised that he was " for it " and promptly reported the facts. He was put under immediate arrest and was called to account the following morning. Fortunately the officer was a fellow Highlander; questions and answers were in Gaelic and when Ranald described the final insult and how he could not stand it any longer and just let the Rooshian have it, the officer exploded with laughter, clapped Ranald on the shoulder and exclaimed " By Gad! you were quite right, and I would do the same myself too!—but I'll have to put you in guard-room for a week all the same." The punishment was lightened, however, by the fact that Colonel M——— called round to see the prisoner every morning, surreptitiously bringing along with him a toothsome bite of food—and a gill of the spirit of the glens! When we read in school the rather prosaic history of the Crimean War and the Siege of Sebastopol we felt a sort of contempt

for the official historian.   But of course, that poor
man did not have the advantage of that knowledge of colourful detail which we of the ceilidh
had.

CHAPTER XI

Angus of the Second Sight.

THERE was another of the ceilidh coterie—Angus—who deserves special mention, for I believe if ever a man had the gift of second sight this man had it. He had eyes that just looked into and clean through you. He had a fine contempt for the ordinary conventions; he might call in to the ceilidh and sit smoking and gazing into the fire for hours without contributing one word to the conversation; then he might get up and leave abruptly with or without a brief *oidhche mhath* (good night). On such occasions it was impossible to say whether or not he was in any degree conscious of what the others were talking about. I am nearly sure he was not for I have often see him after maybe an hour of absolute silence and intense fire-gazing suddenly look up towards the company and, irrespective of whether someone was still talking or not, begin to address them on some subject connected with the supernatural.

Angus openly claimed to have the power of foreseeing events and to have frequently been assisted in the performance of Herculanean tasks by supernatural agencies. When this man began

to talk we youngsters just " froze " in our seats.
The lesson books might still lie open before us
but our every absorptive mental faculty was con-
centrated on the words of the speaker, and shivers
ran up and down our spines as the tale unfolded.
It was usually a story of some supernatural experience of the speaker himself—of knocks which fore-
told deaths; of wandering lights which preceded
national or international calamities; or of phantom
funerals met at certain points of the road. I confess that, even last autumn as I passed one of these
spots at the quiet dark hour of midnight an
involuntary " creep " wriggled up my spine and
seemed to upend the few remaining hairs on the
top of my head.

It is true that most of the tales were of the past,
so that we were not in a position to check their
veracity or the teller's powers of divination, but
there were two incidents for the truth of which I
can vouch.

The first came right closely under my own
observation. I shall merely give the facts and
attempt no explanation—for the simple reason
that I sought diligently for one for years, quite
unsuccessfully.

Angus was a very industrious man. He would
occupy any spare time in reclaiming parts of the
croft which were still in the rough. One November he put in several days reclaiming a rough belt
near the high road. In the process he encountered
a huge boulder buried its own depth in the earth.

Angus dug down and round about it until it was quite exposed. I inspected it closely and made a rough calculation of its measurements and weight. As it was roundish in shape only an approximate weight could be arrived at, but I am sure it weighed not less than two tons and it may have been nearly three. It lay in a pit just its own depth below the ground, *i.e.,* its top was on a level with the surface of the ground and its bottom lay in a hole some five feet deep. One evening at dusk, coming along the road I stopped to talk to Angus who was sitting smoking on the boulder and pleased that he had now fully exposed it. I remarked that of course his next step would be to blast it.

" I will not blast it," he said, curtly.

" Anyhow," I said, " You will have to break it to pieces somehow before you can get it out of that hole."

" I will take it out whole," he said, " and that before to-morrow morning." As he had now assumed that mysterious manner I knew so well, I said nothing further and went home, smiling to myself and certain that the stone would still be there when I passed in the morning. I had had a hard experience of levering boulders out of the ground, and I knew very well that no combination of lever and fulcrum and " purchase " that could be applied to that stone by as many men as could get effectively round it would lift it out of that hole; and Angus was alone.

Next morning at daybreak I passed along by that road again and words are quite inadequate to express my astonishment at seeing the stone lying on the surface of the ground beside the hole and the hole empty! And Angus was standing beside the boulder that now looked even bigger than before. There was an expression of quiet triumph on his face and before I could utter a word he said in Gaelic, " I told you I would do it, and there it is."

" But," I asked, " how on earth did you do it? " He looked me straight through the eyes and said in the way so characteristic of him, " *Thog mi mach i—ach fhuair mi cobhair!* " (" I lifted it out —but I got help! "—meaning from a supernatural source). This incident kept the men of the Glen guessing for the rest of their lives. Close investigation of several possible explanations gave not a ray of light and I leave it at that.

The other incident was told to me by my uncle who was an eye-witness of it, and who hitherto had been sceptical of Angus's claims as a seer—but who, if the subject cropped up ever afterwards, declared that there was " something in it," as he could never forget the Achnasheen incident. Here is the story:

It happened when the Dingwall and Stromferry railway was being built in 1871. A number of people from the Strath were employed in various capacities at the making of the railway. Hundreds of navvies from all over Britain and Ireland were employed there. One day Angus and my uncle were engaged along with a gang of navvies of mixed nationality at a rock-cutting west of Achnasheen station. The navvy gang's conversation was of the choice order usual to that fraternity; but Angus worked in silence and never took any part in the ribald profanity around him. Just before dinner time one day when the language had attained to a deeper degree of profanity and blasphemy than usual, Angus suddenly threw down his pick and started back with an exclamation. All stopped to look at him. He was now gazing intently at the rock-face and perspiring freely. After a few moments he walked to the bank and put on his jacket. He then turned to the gang and said in that quietly dramatic way he had, "You men! instead of using such dreadful language should be saying your prayers, for by this time to-morrow death will be amongst you. I saw blood on the rock!"—and without another word he walked away.

The incident awed even that crowd of toughs for a few minutes, but when they knocked off for dinner they made it the subject of rude jest, and by night had forgotten practically all about it.

But next day at eleven o'clock, while the same gang were working in the same cutting, a "dead" blast exploded in their midst. One man was killed on the spot and another seriously injured, *and the blood of both was on the rock.*

CHAPTER XII

Dark Doings—*Snàth Sgochadh Feithe* (The Spraining String) —Stopping Blood—A sick cow and *Burn Airgid*— Sacrifice of the Black Cockerel—Horror in the Glen— the *Corp-Creadha!*—The Death of Superstition.

In the days of which I write recourse to the Occult was frequent. Should a person sprain a wrist or ankle, or a beast a tendon, a friend went as a matter of course to *Bean Choinnich an Fhidhleir* (Kenny-the-Fiddler's wife), for a *snàth sgochadh feithe*. Elsewhere in this book a full description is given of the making of this wonderful "spraining-string." The string was tied loosely round the damaged limb and he was a brave man who questioned its efficacy! I have personally gone to the old lady for at least a dozen of her famous strings. The first time was for my brother when he fell off a horse and sprained his ankle. The last time was for Kenny Grant's mare's hind leg—a sprained tendon.

Old Ann had the power of "stopping blood"— a most valuable accomplishment. When a school-chum of mine got his foot cut badly with a broken bottle and the thing continued to bleed and bleed —well, the lad who was with him at the time— Johnnie C.—just ran as hard as his legs would carry him to Ann's cottage. Ann immediately

47

" did and said ' something ' " and assured the messenger that the bleeding had now stopped—which, as a matter of fact, it had!   Ann died only about thirty years ago.

Then there was a very old *Cailleach* whom I can just remember—*Mairi Mhor*—who had the rather rare gift of putting the *sian* on a man.   She " treated " Ranald before he went to the Crimean War, and never a scratch did he receive throughout the whole campaign.   Mairi's gift was also resorted to by Calum before he went to the Egyptian war.   Calum had hair-breadth escapes by the dozen and the only hurt he got was a scratch on the ribs from a Dervish spear—but that was not to be wondered at, as I have told in another chapter.

In 1892 my father bought a cow at the Muir-of-Ord Market.   Within a day or two she developed a bad cough.   Soon it was evident that the cow had been " doctored up " for sale and that she was really in a bad state of health.   As usual in such cases—professional veterinary advice being rather expensive—the local " vet." was called in.   Now this man, a crofter in the strath, though an amateur, had undoubtedly a wonderful skill in veterinary science.   Moreover, his skill was ever at the service of his neighbours without fee or reward. In this case Davy tried every likely remedy he could think of.   But the cow grew worse.   He then suggested to my father that, all ordinary cures having failed, he would like to try *Bùrn-Airgid*

(Silver water). My father consented, qualifying the consent with " If it doesn't do any good it can't do any harm."

I was only very young at the time, but, sensing there was something special afoot I determined to see what I could. So, keeping well out of the circle of light shed by the stable lantern which my father carried, this is what I saw and heard. The conversation was all in Gaelic, but for convenience I will render it in English.

Said Davy to my father, " Get me a wooden vessel, a piece of silver money and something of gold."

My father went away and in a few minutes returned with a wooden trough, a half crown and my mother's wedding ring, and handed the lot to Davy.

" Now," said Davy, " half fill the trough with spring water.

My father did so, at the well, and brought it to the byre.

At this stage, on tip-toe with curiosity, I nearly blundered by approaching too close to the scene of operation; but I just managed in time to withdraw from the circle of light. Yet I could clearly see what took place.

Davy dropped first the half crown and then the gold ring into the water. With a stick he stirred the water about. He then passed his hands repeatedly over the vessel in true Hey! Presto! fashion, and muttered a *duan,* of which, I regret,

D

not a word could I make out. Then dipping his hand in the water he carried it, dripping, over above the cow's head and sprinkled her neck with the *bùrn airgid*. He repeated the process until the whole of the spine from head to tail was liberally sprinkled. The while he sprinkled he muttered his *duan* or whatever *Beannachadh* (blessing) it was. Finally, he turned to my father and said those words which will always stick in my memory:

"*Well a Dhomhnuill, mar dian sin feum dhi, cha'n urrainn mise an corr a dheanamh*" (Well, Donald, if that does not do her good I can do no more for her).

The artistic finish to the foregoing would be to record that by morning the cow had quite recovered. A regard for truth, though, compels me to state that when I went to the byre early next morning the cow was dead.

One summer's day, when I was very young, yet able to drive the horses in the harrows, I was employed in that occupation. I was surprised to see a number of people—men and women— dressed in their Sunday best wending their several ways towards a neighbour's house. First I thought it must be for a mid-week prayer meeting; but then I wondered how it was I hadn't heard of such. While still wondering I was further puzzled to see both my own parents leave home, also all dressed up. Now, a country boy resents ongoings like these without knowing the reasons for them. But

I was too far away from anybody to shout and ask what was afoot.

About an hour after the last visitor had disappeared into the neighbour's house the whole lot came out again and skailled solemnly homewards. My parents came towards home and I made sure of being at a point with the harrows where I could intercept and interrogate them regarding such mysterious on-goings. My father merely waved me aside and said, "Ask your mother." But mother was disinclined to divulge anything and the most that I could get out of her was that she "might tell me again." Later that day I wormed it out of her.

"Ach!" she said, "If you must know, we were just trying to do something to help J.'s lassie M."

This girl, by the way, who was about eight years of age, had for two or three years been subject to very distressing fits, and the story my mother told me was as follows:

An old woman of the Glen, wise in certain mystic rites had, after consultation with the child's parents and an elder of the church—a most worthy man—decided that one of these rites should be performed in the hope of effecting the cure of little M., all efforts by the medical profession in that direction having utterly failed.

The first requisite was an all-black cockerel—which must be an "offering." Fortunately an aunt of mine possessed such a cockerel and at once offered it for the occasion.

The next point of material importance was a knowledge of the exact spot on which the wee lassie had had the first fit. This was known to her parents. It happened to be in the lobby of their house. This lobby was at that time floored with Caithness flags. With the requisite material and knowledge assured, invitations were sent to selected neighbours—all known to be very friendly disposed towards the afflicted family—to attend to take part in a semi-sacred semi-sacrificial rite. They met in the parlour. A short religious service of prayer and praise was conducted by the elder. Then one of the Caithness flags was removed with pick and crowbar from its place in the lobby. A hole was dug. The black cockerel with legs tied together, was placed in the hole. The earth was returned so that the cockerel was buried alive. The flag was replaced. A prayer was addressed to the Deity pleading for the removal of His afflicting hand from the house of His servants. The crowd skailed homewards. . . .

How I laughed when I got the story. . . . ! " Really! " I protested, " you don't believe in such nonsense."

" I don't know whether I believe or not," was my mother's reply, " but we were asked to go and we couldn't refuse. Besides, one never knows."

I remained utterly sceptical and waited confidently to hear of the next fit so that I could rub the ridicule into my parents. The opportunity never came. That little girl is now a robust matron with a grown-up family; and never one further seizure did she have since the day of the sacrifice of the black cockerel.

That's a much more artistic finish than the last one, and it, too, has the merit of being true.

Practices involving contact with the occult were usually resorted to only with a benevolent motive —to mend a limb, to cure a disease, to arrest loss of blood; to release a person or animal from evil influences; to confer immunity from bodily injury, etc. It is true that the very necessity for some of these—for the release from evil influences, for instance—implied the existence in the neighbourhood of some people with evil gifts and intentions. One or two I knew were discredited with having and using the evil eye—which caused not a little trouble to man and beast; but such cases were infrequent. That, perhaps, is why the one case of undoubted malevolence in my experience stands out so clearly in my memory.

There was in the glen at that time a certain functionary of much power and influence. To put it mildly, this person was not beloved by the community at large. While still middle-aged he contracted a severe illness and though no hearts would have broken had he been permanently called hence it came as a shock to the glen when it was learned that someone had actually gone the length of positive and active enmity. One evening while two natives were going through a wood and along a burn which ran through it didn't one of them catch sight of something peculiar lying at the edge of a pool and partially covered by overhanging ferns? On closer investigation the men realised that the object was nothing other than a *corp-creadha*. (A monstrous effigy in clay, stuck all over with nails and pins.) It bore an unmistakable likeness too, to the man who was ill. The running water had already caused a considerable wasting of the clay. The news went round the district like wild-fire and there was little doubt in the mind of every native that, had the *corp-creadha* not been discovered—and destroyed—the life of their unbeloved would have ended at the moment when the running water of the burn had disintegrated the last remnant of the gruesome effigy.

In these days of "enlightened" learning, it is a convention to smile in a superior sort of way at the "superstitious" beliefs of our "ignorant" grandparents. The floodlight of scientific research has left no dark eerie corners in which belief in such things as Evil Eye, Witches or Second-sight can survive; and the many occult charms and rites commonly resorted to in the Highlands less than half a century ago are now merely a matter for cultural interest—perhaps! Yet as one knowing the Highlands intimately, and its people and their language I assert that often only lip-service is paid to the modern convention; and that beneath the surface—not much beneath at that—a substantial measure of belief in the old superstitions still survives.

Quite recently, I talked with an old lady in Ross-shire who showed me a small piece of elm twig she had carried for ten years in the pocket of her skirt as a protection for her cow against the evil eye of an unfriendly neighbour. When I smiled and urged it was ridiculous to believe either in the evil eye or in the efficacy of a bit of elm as a precaution she retorted that before she had resorted to the elm twig two cows in succession had " gone wrong " on her—one in the udder, and the other took fits—and I might laugh as I liked but she would carry her elm twig!

CHAPTER XIII

A GLANCE at some of the vital aspects and outstanding events of what I call the Long Trail—
meaning the journey from the cradle to the coffin
—may be of interest. A coffin suggests something
doleful—but that's as it may be; and, to end on
the lighter note I take the coffin end first.

Generally, it may be taken that the Reaper with
the Scythe did not manage to get in his blow at
the inhabitants of the glen till they had reached a
ripe old age. Rarely indeed was it otherwise. In
these circumstances although due and genuine
sorrow was evinced at the passing of an old neighbour and friend there was a certain sensible and
philosophic attitude in regard to the matter which
tended to lighten the grief.

Up till about twenty-five years ago an occasional
" lykehouse " was still " kept." Ten years earlier
the custom was general. That is to say, when a
death occurred a number of neighbours and relations sat up each night with the afflicted family
while the body lay unburied. Nor was the
company by any means a doleful one. Each person

on arrival viewed the corpse and touched its forehead—a precaution against unpleasant dreams—and made some remark that was half of regret yet tinged with happy memories of the departed. Then he or she sat round the fire with the others and joined in general conversation. Never was much *bròn* (wailing) allowed into tone or talk. If the departed formed the topic of conversation at all it was only to touch on events brave or jolly or comical, in which he or she had been the ringleader. An occasional dram was sent round and did its share in achieving the underlying object of the lyke-house—a mutual " cheer-up " in a mutual sorrow—but never have I seen anything approaching drunkenness or conduct in the slightest degree unseemly.

The same can be said of funerals. It would have been a disgrace to bury any old person without at least one dram for all the mourners at the lifting and another at the churchyard—and one or two later at the house, for special friends and relations—but I have never seen an instance in our glen that would give any basis for the well-known joke about the man waking from a drunken sleep in a ditch and being in doubt as to whether his condition had been occasioned by a wedding or a funeral.

Weddings were big affairs in those days. There were no weddings in the church; that for us would have been sheer *mòr-chuis* (swank). Every bride was married from her mother's " room "—the

parlour of the house—or in the little local
" hallie." The neighbours were invited practically *en masse* and all came who could. Presents
were numerous and a good mixture of the orna-
mental and useful. Hens were a special feature—
very sensibly designed towards helping with the
wedding feast. On occasion a present took the
form of a carcase of a sheep or a roast of beef—
very useful too—but hens were the chief victims
of our Hymeneal celebrations. Days before the
great event they were handed in at the door in
pairs and pairs and pairs till a truly amazing total
was sometimes attained.

Before the " Hallie " was built the biggest barn
or granary in the vicinity of the house was
requisitioned for the dance. Of the old-time
dancing I have treated elsewhere in this book.
Here I need only say that dancing reached its
high-water mark at the weddings!

There was a lot of musical talent too, which lay
dormant in a number of people until kindled to
life by the wedding dance and the heart-warming
and courage-inspiring " refreshments " which
accompanied it.

I cannot give the same certificate for sobriety
at the weddings that the funerals earned—but,
truth to tell, a dead-sober wedding was (and is) a
dull affair!

While on the subject of dram-drinking there is
a point I want to make—and emphasise. From
our earliest years we were accustomed to handling

and tasting whisky. Boys of ten years and younger
—aye and girls too—were offered a dram by their
parents on New Year's morning and on other
occasions. They were by custom expected to take
the glass in hand, say "*slainte mhath*" ("good-
health") and just taste the fiery spirit. When
they grew up they were allowed to exercise their
discretion as to the amount taken. I have often
heard it urged that it is highly dangerous to allow
young folks to taste intoxicating liquors on the
ground that it tends to create a liking which is apt
to develop into a crave for drink and so make
undesirable citizens of them in later years. There
may be physiological or pathological facts which
go to support that view. I do not know. But I
do know that of 257 people born in the Glen over
a period of some thirty years—and to 90 per cent.
of whom whisky was freely offered from their very
early days—less than half a dozen reached anything approaching the reprobate stage with drink.

On the other hand I know of several cases where
the custom of early familiarity with whisky
undoubtedly had the effect of influencing a man
towards a strictly temperate life—cases where
youths in their late teens or early twenties for once
failed to guage their "safety mark" and went
ingloriously over the score—to their such intense
mortification that they were on guard against
drunkenness for the rest of their lives.

Nowadays a birth in the glen is a rarity. Not
so in the last thirty years of the nineteenth cen-

tury!   In that time, to 43 mothers were born, as
near as may be, 257 children—an average, by the
way, of six per family.   There was one family with
only one child.   The largest family mustered
eleven juniors.   Families of from five to eight were
the most common.   There was only one childless
married woman.

In the majority of confinement cases a doctor
was not sent for at all.   In the great majority of
cases where a doctor was called in he appeared at
the house hours after the " arrival " and when the
" Howdie " had made all safe for mother and
child.   Quite recently I read in the papers of a
proposal to introduce new legislation which is
intended to ensure that no other than a doctor or
trained midwife shall officiate at a birth.   I do not
quarrel with the wisdom or otherwise of such a
law, but I do wish to state the rather striking fact
that of the 257 children and 43 mothers mentioned
above only three children died at birth and not
one mother died in childbed.

Very probably the natural, healthy life led by
the mothers in the glen—fresh air, plain feeding
and an amplitude of interesting duties—contri-
buted in no small degree to their own and their
offsprings' almost complete immunity from serious
trouble at so critical a time.   But, on reflection, it
seems to me there was more than that in the
explanation.   Amongst country mothers, in those
days at any rate, child-bearing was regarded as a
perfectly natural and normal function, and as

such—assuming ordinary commonsense care and precautions—did not involve them in any really serious danger. They were clear of the paralysing mist of morbid dread and neurotic fears with which the function of child-bearing has come to be surrounded. . . . But I had better get off dangerous ground and let the matter rest on my facts!

CHAPTER XIV

Old *Feills—Feill na Manachainn* (Muir-of-Ord Market)—A
Tale of a Suit—*Feill Chailean* (Colin's Market)—A Day
of Cloudless Pleasure.

In " The Trysting Place " towards the end of this
book a description is given of the Muir-of-Ord
Market—*Feill na Manachainn* as it was sometimes
called. The *Manachainn* had reference to the
Monastery at Beauly near which was the stance of
an older market. Later the market was shifted to
the Muir-of-Ord some two miles farther north and
although the Gaelic name of the new stance was
the *Blàr Dubh,* with many people the old name of
Feill na Manachainn persisted.

The advent of the auction mart sounded the
knell of the " Muir-of-Ord." In the years before
the war it had degenerated to little more than the
selling and swapping of a few superannuated
horses and a fight or two amongst the tinkers. But
in the eighties it was still the Falkirk Tryst of the
north.

I retain one vivid recollection of this market. It
was on a day in June forty-four years ago. The
preceding evening I was thrilled to the marrow
when my mother told me that it had been decided
I should accompany father on the morrow with the

stirks to the Muir-of-Ord market; and that, if the stirks made anything over £6 apiece I would get a new suit! That night gave me my first experience of insomnia.

At five next morning I was up feeding and grooming the stirks. We were off at six on our eleven mile drove. By ten o'clock we were duly stanced on the Muir.

Then came the weary waiting for offers. For nearly two hours not one of the scores of drovers gave us more than a passing look. About noon a big man with a blob nose came along.

" Aye man," said he to my father, " What are ye seekin' for the stirks? "

" Six pounds five shillings apiece," was the reply.

" Ye mean six pounds five shillings for the *two*," came the withering retort as Blob-nose walked away.

An hour later a man with a smug, sickly, sanctimonious smile came along.

" How much for the stirks, good man? "

" Six pounds five shillings apiece."

" You mean five pounds six shillings apiece? "

No reply from my father other than a look of scorn.

Several dealers then came along in quick succession, but the best offer was £5 10/-. Then another dreadful hiatus. We were on the point of starting for home at six o'clock when he of the blob nose reappeared. The nose had by this time acquired somewhat of a carnation colour.

" I'll gie ye six pounds apiece, maister," said he,
" and that's a pound too much."

" Off home with them," was my parent's reply.

Had I been wearing boots my heart would no
doubt have dropped into them.   As it was, it just
seemed to ooze out of me altogether as I headed the
stirks for home.   I had gone maybe a hundred
yards in that direction when Blob-nose bawled,
" Here, Maister!   I'll gie ye yir price but there'll
be a lucks-penny."

I stopped.   My father turned round.   The two
met.   " Haud oot yir haun'," said the drover. Out
went the left palm.   Twelve golden sovereigns
were deliberately counted into it; then two crowns.
One of the crowns was handed back as lucks-penny.
The two principals shook hands.   Like shot I
about-turned the stirks in the direction of their
new owner.

We walked the eleven weary miles home.   I
slept a round and a half of the clock and next week
I got my first real new suit.

One by one the other old *Feills* of Ross-shire
died out.   They were interesting landmarks and
we have nothing quite like them.   Many of them
were associated with some saint or other and no
doubt originally were of a semi-sacred character
although in later years they came to be regarded
merely as stock markets and finally degenerated
into holidays where Cheap Johns, merry-go-rounds
and sweetie stalls held sway.

Feill-Mhàrtainn had a wide vogue, marking as

it did the Feast of All Souls on the first day of November—*Oidhche a' Shamhuinn*. The *feill* itself is no more, but there is still a relic of old-time ploys amongst country boys on that night—the night of Hallowe'en.

Feill Mhìcheil was another of the big markets but there was a good deal of variation in the actual day of observing it in different localities. Practically not a vestige of *Feill Mhìcheil* remains in Scotland; but Michaelmas is still one of the English quarter-days.

In the spring of the year—2nd February to be exact—*Feill Bhrìde* was celebrated. It was still quite a feature of the year too. There is still occasional reference in Scottish farm leases to *Feill Bhrìde* as Candlemas and it has prominence as Candlemas in the English and the Roman Catholic Churches.

Then there were the more local markets—*Feill a' Pheabair* (The Pepper Market) was one; it died out in Ross-shire in the seventies.

Feill Èideachan was originally the special market at which the women bought ribbons and laces and such finer articles of apparel as they could not weave at home, and at which the men got themselves properly equipped with the " harness of war "—body armour, shirts of mail, etc.—for the purveying of which the smiths and armourers were in attendance and did a roaring trade. But *Feill Èideachan* had lost all its original significance long before my time.

E

Feill Seònaid (Janet's or Jessie's Market) was another that is just outwith my recollection but which was a favourite with the previous generation. Who exactly Seonaid was I could never discover but her market held long sway in the north and did not quite die out till the early eighties of the last century.

But, so far as the youngsters of forty to fifty years ago were concerned there was only one survival that counted, and that was *Feill Chailean* (Colin's Market) the very mention of whose name revives a flood of youthful memories. It was held on the second Tuesday of August—by which time, by the way, the blaeberries should be at their best—and how our excitement grew as *Latha Feill Chailein* approached! For weeks in advance every penny was a prisoner, to be liberated on that great day. I have often wondered if any bairns ever got greater pleasure out of less coin of the realm than we did at *Feill Chailein*!

We could scarcely sleep the night before. By six o'clock in the morning as many as two or three dozen of us—boys and girls—dressed in the best togs we could muster, including boots as a concession to town gentility, would start off for Dingwall whose High Street would be lined with stalls on which would be heaped such an assortment of toys and " goodies " as we would only see at *Feill Chailein* and in our dreams.

Some of the keepers of the stalls might be strangers but many came there year after year. In this category Harry-the-Jew's Wife reigned supreme. She was old when I first saw her but she never seemed to grow older. As to form, she was ample and ugly, but she had a kindly streak in her, too, and her goodies were the best on the *feill*. Her *pièce de resistance* was a yellow candy-rock that we knew by a euphonious if somewhat inelegant name of our own. At the start of the day there would be a veritable mountain of this candy-rock on the end of her stall. But customers came in queues. As each came along the old lady chipped a piece off with a little iron hammer and handed it over, *sans* paper, *sans* palaver in return for the tendered copper. By evening the mountain would have vanished.

Our funds were never great in those days. If the older ones had command of a shilling on the morning of the great day they were passing rich. The younger ones ran down to mere pennies. But with judicious selection it was wonderful what a few pence would purchase. With eightpence at *Feill Chailein* I have bought: —

A pistol	1d.
A box of caps	½d.
A watch	2d.
3 sugary biscuits	1d.
1 lump of the famous candy-rock . .	½d.
2 minutes on a swing	2d.
A fourth-share in a bottle of lemonade .	1d.

—and a day of cloudless pleasure that only a boy can buy.

CHAPTER XV

Days of Independence—*Lath a' Mhàil* (Rent-Day)—Gugan
and his Donkey.

In these days of distressing unemployment it may
seem odd to urge the need for holidays. But there
is a world of difference between a real holiday and
enforced idleness; and even now there must be
many urgently in need of relaxation from the
daily round, the common task that eternally keeps
their noses to the grindstone.

For most of the women in the glen, from the
day they were married till the day they were laid
to rest in the old Churchyard anything in the
nature of a real respite was practically unknown.
It must not be inferred from this that on the
whole they lived unhappy lives; far from it; for
their's was that life of service to others in which
the greatest happiness is to be found. But oh!
how they must have longed for an occasional week
off the chain, those brave self-sacrificing women.

For the men, apart from New Year's Day, the
two great holidays of the year were the day of the
games and rent-day—*Lath a' Mhàil.*

The games afforded to the men an opportunity
of putting on their Sunday suits, a real enjoyable
day witnessing, or taking part in, the various

68

sports and a trouble-banishing spree at the finish. They were held in the district cow-park, and for the twenty-odd cows that were put to summer grazing there the games-day was a holiday too; for on that day they were sent to another field where for the first hour they were happy in the exercise of true bovine curiosity sniffing out the mysteries of a stale ditch and later gloried gastronomically in the fresher pasture which the new field afforded.

Another tenant of the games park was Jeannie—a donkey belonging to an old character who went by the name of Gugan. For weeks Jeannie would be as docile and well-behaved as the best lady-visitor at the Strath. But that was only part of her guile, just to allay suspicion and blot out public recollection of her past misdeeds. Then when Jeannie reckoned that the cow-owners' recollections were sufficiently dim, she played her joke.

In the dead of night she would nibble and chew the rope with which the gate had been tied as an extra " safety," and by dawn would have the knots untied. Then with uncanny skill she shot back the bolt and pushed the gate open. The visitors at the Strath that morning would be entertained by the appearance of a number of cows strolling in bands in front of the shops and wandering round the Pump-room. Altogether Jeannie's joke never failed to cause a degree of annoyance to the cow-owners and amusement to others that must, I am sure, have given herself an impish satisfaction; for, having liberated the cows, she herself remained innocently in the park.

The day of the Highland Gathering was one of the most popular of the year. There we could see the great Donald Dinnie's Herculanean prowess with hammer and cabar, and our then local star— still very much in the flesh—Kenny Whitton, with his extraordinary athletic versatility. Then there was Dunkie MacDonald, another " local " who had broken the world's record vault at the Paris Exhibition, and could still, with the help of a drop of courage which he deliberately sipped from a " bottlie " kept in his pocket for the purpose, usually out-vault them all.

Another of the outstanding ones was Merchant, yon little high-jumper from Aberdeen, who used to give us a laugh by walking back under his own jump wearing a tile hat on his head!—and there still would be inches to spare.

But not a few of us went to the games to satiate our music-starved souls (the clergy frowned on all but psalm tunes) with the flood of melody which poured from the pipes of young Johnnie MacDonald and Willie Ross who were winning prizes even then—and who now, as Scotland's veteran Pipe-Majors, are universally acclaimed two of the greatest descendants of MacCrimmon.

For the boys of the glen only *Feill Chailein* rivalled the day of the games in the whole year's round.

A boy might pay his entrance money like the

rest, but that was only when he was in funds—or was unfortunate. There was a nice shading of honesty—or the reverse—about this matter of paying to get in. When a boy hadn't the price he just didn't go. He went to the woodie for a feed of geans instead, and pretended he preferred geans to games. When he had the price of admission and no more he would walk in as bold as brass, not by the regular entrance but from the far side of the park. He selected the moment for advance, though, with a nice regard to the position of the patrolling Bobby. If Robert had an eye to promotion or was afflicted with conscience-scruples in the way of abstract honesty, the ruse seldom worked; in which case our hero would advance straight towards the arm of the law and proffer the price of admission—pleading ignorance of the rule that admission was by the gate only! But if Dame Fortune smiled and he was left with the shilling to regale himself at the stalls his conscience salve was the same as that of the respectable citizen who goes off the street cars without paying his fare— nobody asked him to pay!

On *Lath a' Mhàil* every man donned his Sunday suit, paid his due, took off his dram from the factor and looked the world in the face. And if he took several more drams and indulged with his fellows in a hilarious and belated home-coming—what of it? *Lath a' Mhàil* was his day of independence.

It was in this spirit that a band of worthy neighbours I remember so well, having " cleared their

feet with the factor " would repair to the *tigh-osda*
(Inn) and in the course of a day of unshadowed
bliss, consume as much *uisge-beatha* (whisky) as
ultimately led their physical feet into obvious
trouble.   The metamorphosis which John Barley-
corn effected, changing men of staid, reticent,
rather serious cast into happy-go-lucky creatures
bubbling over with mirth and wit and humour,
was something to marvel at and highly interesting.   It was a gradual process; each dram did
its little bit to put the *bodach* out of them, until
at last, one by one, they were indeed:

"O'er a' the ills o' life victorious."

The very atmosphere of that day seemed to affect
Donncha Beag; the frown flitted from his face
before the first dram.   Not so with *Fearchar Fada*
who had a head "like cast iron" that stood the
subtle influences amazingly. But when at last this
stronghold did succumb it was no half surrender!

Thus elevated and equipped—for each took a
bottle in his pocket—it was only half-a-crown—
late in the evening the gang would start their
homeward way.   It was no Marathon, that journey
home; it must have been about the record in slow
motion.   Points in morals and philosophy had to
be discussed.   There were fine theological values
to adjust.   And that necessitated sitting down—
which they did frequently—at the side of the road.

By midnight they would arrive at the road-end
where the first break in the party must take place.

That called for a special sederunt; just a wee *deoch an doruis*; much protestation of friendship and *" Mo Rùn Geal Dìleas"* (" My Faithful Fair One ") from *Dònull a' Chiobair* if he had arrived at the singing stage. *Lath a' Mhàil* was the only day in the year that *Dònull* was ever heard to sing; but on that day he put a wealth of love and longing into that beautiful Gaelic song that gave the key to the reason for his single state. Long years before there had been a *" Rùn "* in his life. She had not proved *" dìleas";* she had gone away and married another. But never once did *Dònull* think or say a hard word of her; and every year, on *Lath a' Mhàil* he paid loving tribute to her memory.

As the ceremony had to be repeated at each parting of the ways it told rather heavily on Iain Dearg and " Maoilean " who had farthest to go. Indeed that pair usually spent what remained of that night in a fashion from which worldly care was gloriously excluded—the end of a perfect day!

" Shocking! " exclaims your rigid moralist. Is it, indeed? Well, maybe it is; and maybe that is what our heroes themselves thought of it in the grim realities of next morning—a sore head and a sorrowful wife. But is that all? Is there no other side to it? Does not some psychological and physiological lesson lie somewhere in the conduct of these otherwise most worthy of men? Is not excessive hilarity the inevitable result of excessive monotony? Can you blame your dog if he makes a riotous frolic of his own day off the chain?

CHAPTER XVI

Smuggling—A drop o' the *Creutair*—Guest of His Majesty—
Safety First.

LARGELY a fruit of the " Forty-five," the rigorous
efforts towards the suppression of illicit distilling
were never too popular with the people of the
Highlands. The natives of the north very naturally resented that drastic interference with their
liberty; just as they resented having to encase their
legs in ridiculous tubes of cloth instead of leaving
them bare to the winds of heaven in the kilt. Con-
sequently only in the eyes of the law was it ever
held to be a crime to cheat the gauger. In fact,
the man who succeeded in making his own drop of
the *creutair* despite the vigilance of the gauger
and his staff was regarded rather as a hero in public
estimation.

Of course, that spirit is now quite dead. . . . eh?
Oh! yes, of course. . . . maybe . . . But maybe
there are two or three places that I know
of, far up by the burnside in the higher corries,
where the " worm " is not yet rusty and the *poit-
dhubh* has no holes in its bottom . . . maybe . . .
but I better no' be saying! And maybe the story
that follows is just a figment of the imagination .. ?

Quite recently I was staying over the week-end

74

" somewhere in the North." The gaugers had
been busy for days searching the neighbourhood.
One of them spoke to me in the village street. He
told me all about their activities; they were hot on
the track of the smugglers. While we were talking
an old friend of mine came along. We exchanged
courtesies in the Gaelic. Then I asked him what
he and his neighbours were doing at —— to keep
the men of the knickerbockers so busy.

" For the love of heaven," said he in the Gaelic,
" watch what you are saying! Do you know who
is standing beside us? "

" Fine that," said I, " but the poor *creutair*
hasn't a word of the language."

" Are you certain? " he enquired.

" Quite," I assured him. Then I added, " He
tells me they have given all of you such a fright
that not one will dare go near the bothy again this
summer."

On hearing this, my friend looked at the sky as
if he were searching for signs of the weather;
then, " If himself is of that opinion let him continue it," said he; " but if yourself could be doing
with a drop of the right stuff, maybe I could get
it for you to-night! —and maybe he did!

And maybe I know an old blacksmith who is an
artist at shaping certain " utensils " and in giving
them an aged appearance so that when they are
judiciously distributed and " hidden " in the moss,
and when they are subsequently " discovered " by
an " honest native " who reports the find to the

authorities, their reward value is considerable. Maybe . . . just maybe. One has to be very canny about these matters.

But my next story is an old one and no harm can come of telling it. I can vouch for its truth too.

Just over a hundred years ago there lived on the Heights of Strathpeffer one John Macdonald. He was then about forty years of age. For many years John had kept two smuggling bothies going alternately. One was in *Coire 'Bhothain* and the other at the *Leth-allt* near *Cnoc na Bainnse*. He always played a lone hand thus avoiding the usual pitfall of the smuggler—a babbling confederate. So that not a breath of suspicion blew his way and all might have continued well had not a gamekeeper by an unlucky chance one day actually walked through the roof of the *Coire 'Bhothain* bothy and discovered John redhanded at his hobby. He was an unfriendly gamekeeper that; he lodged information with the authorities at Dingwall.

After trial John was duly sentenced to be detained for a period of six weeks as an unwilling guest of His Majesty King William IV. John's wife walked to Dingwall every other day bringing food for the prisoner. A fortnight went by without incident. Then John had a brain-wave. The old jailor was well known to favour the cup that cheers; in fact he was possessed of a chronic and insatiable thirst—and on that John gambled—and won.

During the remaining four weeks of the sentence there was observed a gentleman's agreement whereby every evening after dark John's cell door was unlocked. John then proceeded by a quiet route to the *Cnoc na Bainnse* bothy and there worked strenuously and in complete safety until returning dawn warned him it was time to make for his prison again; which he did—bringing with him in liquid form the price of the old jailor's complicity.

As John's son put it to me, " The safest smuggling my father ever did was that time he was in Dingwall Jile."

CHAPTER XVII

It is late September. Once again the bloom is off the heather; the grouse are " packing," and the *Sasunnach* sportsmen treking south.

What an interesting interlude this annual visit to the Highlands must be in the lives of not only the " gentry " themselves but also of their retinue of servants, male and female! All thoroughly enjoy themselves, although indeed they never quite manage to grasp the educational and intellectual calibre of the Highland gillies and gamekeepers and other natives with whom they come in contact.

The truth is that before these *Sasunnaich* come north they cherish the usual *Sasunnach* delusion that Highlanders are an ignorant, semi-barbarous people, in kilts and red whiskers. *Na Creutairean bochd!*—and they never get thoroughly to realise how much the boot is on the other foot. Further evidence of the inability of the *Sasunnach* to understand the Highlander is found in the ineradicable belief of the average shooting tenant that the average crofter is an inveterate poacher. That, of course, is absurd. The great majority of crofters have a feeling of sympathy for the usually impecunious laird and are very pleased that the poor man should make the most of his shootings.

Hares and rabbits on the croft are the crofter's to kill as he likes, of course. Moreover, all sensible lairds, knowing the damage hares and rabbits can cause to corn and turnip crops, are glad to see such pests rigorously kept under. But for feathered game like grouse, pheasants and partridges the majority of crofters have no use at all. Apart from any other consideration such fluffy things are bothersome to prepare and cook!

I'm not saying, though, but that once in a while in an amateurish sort of way, some of us might indulge the primordial instinctive love of the chase. For the pursuit of game is older than man-made laws. In every male, to a greater or less degree it is an inherited instinct, the occasional indulgence of which, even if running counter to the law, gives a peculiar joy to the individual. In saying this, I am no mere theorist; fine do I remember the thrill of the illicit hunt. The advent of a new gamekeeper was but added piquancy—a gravy to my grouse.

It was our laird—confound him!—who put an effective end to my poaching (on his estate) over thirty years ago. For what did he do but invite every tenant with a gun to a day's shooting! It was the first time that had been done in our experience and you would scarcely believe how greatly some two score of us appreciated that invitation. Hitherto, our opinion as loyal Land-Leaguers of the laird, had he known it, would not have involved him in any expense in the way of larger sized hats. And this invitation was in a way quite embarrassing! It was all very well to cherish a somewhat hostile attitude towards a laird whose relationships with the smaller tenants were of that aloof and condescending order so charac-teristic of lairds in general, but what was to be our attitude towards this man who not only gave us some good days' sport, but extended generous hospitality to boot? For those few days at anyrate we were as man to man, or, rather, we were a band of brother hunters with equal chances in the chase, eating food out of the same panniers and drinking drams out of the same flask.

Many a time since then have I wondered if the laird ever fully realised how much more effective than a dozen gamekeepers were those delightful days of camaraderie.

Ali Dubh was the one in our glen who came nearest to the amateur artist in poaching. He had an uncanny knowledge of the ways of the wild. For him it was a positive pleasure to pit his craft and guile against the wariness of beast or bird or fish.

As a wee fellow I was one of Ali's worshippers and favourites. Occasionally he would condescend to initiate me into the wiles of the game.

As his name implied, Ali's colouring was black
—beard as black as a crow. He was tall and lean,
and lithe as a monkey. Even with age his wiry
frame refused to carry an ounce of adipose. Ali
was the only man I ever knew who could catch a
hare by " circling " her. Should he, when walking
over a lea field spot a hare lying snug in her tuft
of grass some twenty yards ahead, he never made
the mistake of stopping to look or otherwise indi-
cating that he had seen her. Oh no! That
would have set her off on the instant. So Ali
just glided into a trot, circling the hare.

Round and round he went, gradually lessening
the circle and accelerating the pace. Puss would
stare this way and that, not sure which way to
break and clearly more than half hypnotised by
the now swift gyrations of her hereditary enemy.
Nearly always she hesitated too long. With terrific
force and unerring aim, Ali—now circling on a
five yard radius or so—let fly the shortish stick he
usually carried; and ten-to-one there would be
hare soup in the house to-morrow.

That sounds quite easy, but try it! Many a
time I did, and the hare would be off before I
completed the first lap. There was some mesmeric
quality about Ali Dubh which I did not possess.

Seldom did Ali use the gun. When he did use
it he never wasted powder or shot. But there was
an inconvenient advertisement in the noise of a
gun; besides, it was a crude method compared with
—say—the artistry of his grouse-catching plan.

F

It would be late in October. The harvest would be over—at least it would be all in except for a few stooks which Ali (most unfortunately!) hadn't managed to cart home. Soon the grouse would be sure to discover these stooks. Maybe only half a dozen of them came the first time, but with the true sociability of the aviary they informed the pack of the rare feast which could be had for the pecking. Next day at dawn the stooks would be literally covered with grouse.

And so they would be again the following morning. But then a queer thing happened. A grouse would quietly disappear between two sheaves into the middle of a stook; then another and another in quick succession until maybe a score had mysteriously vanished. And then, to the wild alarm of the birds still feeding on the outside of the stook, Ali would crawl out from its inside— where he had ensconced himself an hour before dawn. With deft fingers he had drawn by the leg bird by bird to its doom!

I found that one much easier than catching the hare.

Then sometimes Ali would be solicitous for the partridges. That would be in the hard frost and snowy days of winter when the poor things had difficulty in picking up a decent meal. Ali, the good Samaritan, would scatter three or four handfuls of barley near some hedge or bushes or stacks which the partridges were likely to visit during the night or early morning. How the poor hungry birds gobbled up that grain! So Ali continued his hospitality for two or three nights. By the fourth night there would be a veritable partridge jamboree, and if you went along early next morning you would get the laugh of your life, for there would be perhaps a score of paitricks as tight as lords, laughing and turning somersaults and with a devil-may-care look in their eye! But they could neither fly nor run away. So you took the poor things home to the fire. . . . Oh! I forgot to explain that an accident had happened to that last night's feed of barley; it had spilt into a bowl of whisky the day before and had lain there for eight hours before Ali remembered to take it out!

But Ali was just an amateur. Finlay was a professional; to what profound depths his cunning went I can only surmise. Finlay was not a crofter; he lived in the town. He was over middle age when first I remember him and continued to an old age actively engaged in the only profession he ever really loved. Over a period extending to nearly sixty years his total appearances before the sheriff on poaching charges must have constituted a record. But what is the good of prosecuting a poacher anyway? Whatever corrective effect fines or imprisonment may have on the average transgressor of the law, to the real poacher they are only a temporary deterrent. This fact is tacitly acknowledged by those sensible judges who invariably allow the poaching delinquent so many days in which to pay the fine. In nine cases out of ten the wind is raised as a result of a more successful poaching expedition than the last one.

The most dramatic incident in Finlay's experience took place some twenty years before I can remember and while he was still a young man. Often did I hear my Uncle Sandy tell the story.

This uncle was grieve on a farm some two miles to the south of the town. One September morning at five o'clock, Sandy as usual was first afoot and seeing that everything was right about the steading. Suddenly into the barn came Finlay in a dreadful state of perspiration and fear. Quickly he told his tale. The previous night while poaching in the woods he was surprised by the gamekeeper. There was a bit of a scuffle. Finlay's gun was accidentally discharged. One of the keepers was killed. (This proved to be incorrect—he was badly wounded but recovered). The alarm had been raised. The police and a band of volunteers had been hunting Finlay from cover to cover all night; but in the dark which preceeds the dawn he had managed to shake them off for a bit. But they would be there soon. Sandy must hide him in the straw and tell the pursuers when they came that he had seen a man disappear into the wood beyond. Into the middle of a huge heap of straw crawled Finlay. Almost immediately along came the hunt. Poor Uncle Sandy!—who in the matter of lies was about on a par with George Washington. But he told a whopper that time—tho' indeed it was not without a lean to the side of virtue. Off went the pursuit into the next wood.

Finlay lay in hiding and was secretly fed by this worthy uncle of mine for three days. Then he headed for the south—not by the high-road we may be sure. Inside a month a stalwart young man (now clean-shaven instead of wearing the beard which men in their early twenties then affected) offered himself for recruitment at the Edinburgh Police office. By what name he went I know not but his physique was so outstanding that he was enrolled forthwith. Next day the smart recruit was on Princes Street in company with an old hand who was showing him round. At the Mound the older policeman took a photograph out of his pocket and handed it to Finlay.

"Here, young fellow," said he, "get your blinkers on to that and if ever you see a man with a face to fit that photo, arrest him. There's promotion there—for you and me."

Finlay took the photo. He looked at it long and hard, taking in its every line and expression—and particularly the beard. He then put it carefully in his pocket.

"Right," said he, never batting an eye, "I think I would know that fellow anywhere"—and well he might!!

For nearly two years Finlay patrolled the streets of Edinburgh as one of its most promising young policemen—diligently searching, we may presume, for the "wanted" Ross-shire poacher whose photograph he carried in his pocket. This is like the story of the sick cow; it has a poor ending. Finlay did *not* finish his career as Chief Constable of Edinburgh.

After nearly two years of meritorious service with the Edinburgh Police, and when the new Finlay might reasonably have hoped that all traces of the old one were safely obliterated, like a bolt from the blue came disaster. A youth from the north joined the Police at Edinburgh. This creature happened to have seen the old Finlay on more than one occasion. He was an observant skunk, keen on promotion. Following a report by him, Finlay was arrested, tried and convicted. The next nine months of his life he spent in durance vile; and the remaining sixty years of it as the most inveterate poacher I ever knew—a super-artist in his profession.

CHAPTER XVIII

In the eyes of the city artisan whose judgment is
based on the *seaps* (guzzles) of butter, cream, fresh
eggs and heather honey incidental to a summer's
holiday, life on the croft is apt to appear in roseate
colours. To the crofter and his family, conscious
of the drudgery of mucking byres, the heartbreak
of a wet harvest and the pain of pulling turnips
on a frosty morning, the colours are apt to be drab.
As usual the truth lies between the two extremes.
While the life is not all the cream and honey
existence imagined by summer visitors, the crofter
is much better off than he himself knows or cares
to admit.

Often I have been asked the question, " But
what *is* a croft worth to the crofter? How much
does it contribute to the livelihood of the family? "
Usually I answered the question evasively because
it did not permit of a brief or definite reply. The
answer depended—as still depends—of course, on
the size and sort of croft, and the man in charge;
and even more particularly, perhaps, on the wife
in charge of the man in charge!

In our strath the crofts varied in extent from one acre to fifty acres, and the rents from less than £1 to £30.

Seventeen of them were too small to maintain a horse. At the other extreme were a dozen crofters who kept " a pair." The middle-sized ones kept one horse only, and " paired up " for ploughing, etc.

As may be surmised, only the biggest type of croft was sufficient to provide an adequate living for the family; and seldom did the occupiers of the large-sized croft resort to " outside " labour. While, as already indicated, the return from the croft varied with many factors, the usual financial statement for a well-worked place of the largest type in the " eighties " would be very much like this: —

INCOME.

From sale of			6 six-quarter old cattle at £10	£60	0	0
,,	,,	,,	20 lambs at 25/- . . .	25	0	0
,,	,,	,,	50 hogs (wintered only) at 25/-	62	10	0
,,	,,	,,	4 fat pigs at 40/- . . .	8	0	0
,,	,,	,,	½ foal (one each alternate year at £10) . .	5	0	0
,,	,,	,,	40 Quarters Oats at 18/- .	36	0	0
,,	,,	,,	4 Tons of Potatoes at £3 .	12	0	0
,,	,,	,,	6 Tons Hay at £3 . . .	18	0	0
,,	,,	,,	120 doz. Eggs at 8d. . . .	4	0	0
,,	,,	,,	Butter, Crowdie and Sundries	5	0	0
			Total Cash Income . .	£235	10	0

EXPENDITURE.

Rent and Rates	£30	0	0
Guano and Bone Meal	6	0	0
Artificial Feeding Stuffs	5	0	0
Grass and Glover Seeds	4	0	0
Smiddy	6	0	0
Ironmonger (for Scythes, hoes, nails, oil, etc.)	3	0	0
Saddler (for major harness, repairs, reins, etc.)	2	0	0
50 lambs bought for wintering at 12/6 . .	31	5	0
2 bought-in calves at £2	4	0	0
4 young pigs at 10/-	2	0	0
Stock service fees	3	0	0
Halflin's wages	14	0	0
Depreciation of implements (against renewals)	10	0	0
Average annual loss by death in stock . .	10	0	0
Sundries	5	0	0
Total Cash paid out . .	£135	5	0

This, deducted from the total cash income of £235, 10/-, left for the family maintenance, say, £100. But in addition to that there was the value of home produce consumed or used by the family, including wool, made into tweed for clothing. Taking a family of six—*i.e.*, father, mother, and four resident children—I put five shillings per head per week as a fair figure. That works out at a total of seventy-eight pounds per annum, giving for the family maintenance in cash and kind a total of £178 in the year.

A further important consideration was that no house-rent was payable; and yet another, that fuel could be had from the moss for the making.

On a middle-sized place the cash sales would be proportionally somewhat less. Those on a £12 croft would approximate a total of . £100 0 0

But a halflin would not be required, so that the total pay-out per annum would be around . . £56 0 0

Leaving a credit Cash Balance of . £44 0 0

The value of home produce consumed and used would be practically the same as in the other case £78 0 0

Which left for the man and his wife and family to live on . . £122 0 0

in addition to the advantages of no house rent and free fuel. In these circumstances, with a view to improving the family financial position—advanced education for at least one of the family was an ambition in most homes—it was usual for the crofter himself, or members of the family while still very young, to engage in " outside " work that offered. Carting for building contractors, thinning and pulling turnips, haying and harvesting for neighbouring farmers, " Gillie " work with the local shooting tenant, ploughing for horse-less neighbours, etc., etc.

In the case of the very small crofts the man-of-the-house was usually a tradesman—masons and joiners predominated—there was an occasional tailor and shoemaker. In our strath the last weaver died before I was old enough to remember him. Even on a croft so small that only a cow, a pig and hens could be kept, and where the " shift " was as little as one acre, the home contribution, consisting as it did of milk, butter, crowdie, eggs, potatoes, chickens, as much as five or six bolls of oat-meal and some very good ham, was very considerable; was, indeed, so considerable as to leave any fear of real poverty entirely out of the question. I never see the professional trained economist trying to reduce the value of a croft to figures or hear lectures on microbes, but I think of *Anna 'Ghobhainn.*

Anna lived her long life in blissful ignorance of all the rules of the hygienist. Not since her mother washed her as a baby did Anna have a bath except that involuntary one on that memorable occasion when, crossing the river on her way home from the peats in the fading light, she stepped on a lump of river-froth which she mistook for a stone and we had some difficulty in hauling her out. The extent of her daily ablutions was limited to her hands and face. Yet kindly neighbours who " prepared " the body when, at the age of ninety-two, Annie's cheery soul at last took flight, for years recalled the " blue-white skin, as beautiful as a child's."

Her bedroom window—which contained one of those " knotty " panes that produced the queerest distortions—was never once opened since it had been put in by Iain Donn nearly a hundred years before Anna was born; and that for the simple reason that Iain, unaffected by modern microbic theories, intended it only for the dual purpose of letting in the light and keeping out the cold. Yet Anna had a vigour of lung and peach-bloom complexion at eighty that few flappers, sleeping under the most modern hygienic conditions, can boast.

Her old brown teapot sat eternally stewing in the hot ashes of a peat fire that rarely died out, and the tanin content of the black brew must have far exceeded the danger point of the toxicologist; but neither Anna's teeth nor intestines seemed a whit the worse.

Anna died before the days of the Old Age Pension but she never accepted charity. From her visible means of support—the produce of a score of hens and an acre of land—a dietetic economist would no doubt prove to his own satisfaction by an elaborate process of calculation and reasoning that Anna could not possibly survive for more than a few months—but he would be wrong.

Yes, so far as supporting a family is concerned there is a *plus* factor in the economics of even a very small croft which it is impossible to reduce to figures.

While on the subject of economics it may be as well to add a word on the matter of food in conjunction with the daily round. Here is a typical case:

In winter the family reveille was around 7 a.m. The wife lit the kitchen fire—often that was merely a matter of reviving the peat embers that had smouldered all night—and set the porridge on the fire to cook the while she milked the cows, fed the pigs and hens and did some general choring.

Before breakfast, the man and one or two of the boys fed the cows, stirks and horses, mucked out byre and stable and tidied the place generally.

Breakfast at 8 o'clock:—
Porridge—with creamy milk.
Tea.
Oat-cakes, Girdle Scones, Butter (eggs too
    scarce and dear in winter).

After breakfast and "The Books," those of school age were got ready—with as much joy then as now—for that tyrannical institution. There was no road to the school; we just went through fields, over dykes and fences and down by the side of a wood.

Into school at 10. Play hour 1-2. Out at 4. home at 5.

As we set off in the morning each carried in the "bag" the "piece" and bottle of milk that was to sustain throughout the day. There were occasional big days when loaf-bread or a cookie figured in the piece, but normally it consisted of generous slabs of oat-meal bannock cemented together with butter or crowdie or both.   A healthy appetite is a wonderful sauce.   It was a hard job holding up the piece till the play hour and what survived till then got the shortest of short shrifts.

Meantime, at home, weather permitting, ploughing was proceeded with, or pulling and driving of turnips.   In stormy weather threshing and the feeding of beasts were the main activities. In the present day of oil-engine driven mills when the straw required for a week can be threshed in an hour it is scarcely possible to imagine the demand on time made by threshing with the flail.

Thump, thump, whack!

Thump, thump, whack!   Even yet I can recall the dull song of the flail going on and on and on . . . What a relentless tyrant that implement was!

By noon the wife would have the dinner ready for those at home.   Do not imagine that that is all she had done since breakfast-time!   I have often tried to recall in detail just what the croft wife did in her long and active day but have always given it up as hopeless.   But of this I am sure: that between baking, washing, milking, cooking, churning, sewing, darning, mending, tending hens and pigs and calves and not infrequently giving a hand with field work, she was unquestionably the busiest person I have ever encountered. And with it all, she was usually the embodiment of health and good spirits.

Dinner: —
Potatoes—boiled in their skins.
Salt herrings—from a barrel laid at the
    beginning of winter.
Tea.
Oatcake, butter.

The meal after the bairns came home was
usually a repeat of dinner but it should be
emphasised perhaps that a lot of milk was consumed by everybody.

Almost invariably on Sunday there was a broth
and beef dinner plus milk pudding de luxe
(because of eggs and cream), plus tea.

Throughout the week, too, there was a surprising variety of relief from the salt-herring diet.
Scarcely a week passed without a hare or rabbit
being caught. There was always a hen or chicken
available. Seasonally, magnificent fresh herrings
were procurable as well as " Kessocks " and
" garvies." Then in spring when eggs were plenti-
ful and cheap, we ate eggs by the half dozen.

In addition to any garden fruit there was
abundance of wild rasps, brambles, and blaeberries;
and in our case the rather rare and delectable
Oidhreag. This fruit rather resembles in form
the loganberry. It grows on a strawberry-like
plant amongst the heather and rarely fructifies
below the 2000 ft. altitude. One of the special
days in the strath was that day towards the end of
July when we went to gather the *Oidhreagan*.

Natives home on holiday looked forward to that day. I have seen as many as thirty of us set off in the morning with ample provisions and pails and baskets, climb for three hours towards our favourite corrie, and in four hours more fill our pails and baskets to the brim with rich red *Oidh-reagan* that made jelly with a sort of honey flavour. . . . Oh yes. Looking back over our menu of those days it seems to me we fared not so badly.

CHAPTER XIX

Hell Fire.

THERE is usually a conventional decorum observed in any reference to the religious life of our grandparents in the Highlands; their piety is always referred to as profound. Yet as one who has spent all his youth and the early years of his manhood right in the thick of it, I fear there is something of the enchantment of distance in that view.

Of religion, so-called, we had a surfeit; but to an unbiased mind the form and dogma of it seemed of greater importance in the eyes of devotees than the tolerance and charity of thought and action which a religion should stand for.

That most of my old neighbours were sincere in their views I do not for a moment deny; but their religion, in both its theoretical and practical aspects was but the reflection of their spiritual teachers' views, and in all conscience these, as a rule, were sombre enough to satisfy the most rigid Calvinist.

It was a cold, uncharitable creed they preached which grudged any joy in life except what could be extracted from gloom. Their doctrine of " predestination " weighted us with a sense of the

G

futility of effort. Present-day ministers who are puzzled at their empty pews can console themselves with the reflection that they are suffering from an inevitable reaction to the morbid ministrations of their professional grandfathers whose dominant note was Hell-fire.

No description of life in a crofting community of the eighties of last century would be complete without some reference to the ever-burning furnace—provided by the Deity whose chief attribute was Love—for the eternal chastisement of sinners.

And I am an authority on Hell. It and all its lurid details were branded on my soul from my tenderest years. I can never forget, or remember without a shudder, the first word-picture of this dread place that a "minister of God" with all the solemnity which that profession then bestowed, so graphically disclosed to my horrified mind at the tender age of some five years.

It wasn't a mere reference to some dire place of punishment. Oh no! With unction he condescended on detail. It was a bottomless yawning hole with a red-and-blue lowe licking into every crannie of it, with the Devil in control of lesser devils whose sole function was to grab sinners and throw them into the hottest corner and roast them and roast them for ever and ever more!

It was this never-ending aspect of the torture that appalled me. It came to my mind that if I got only one short plunge into the fire and was then allowed to jump out and into a pool of cold water it would be bad enough, but bearable. But no fear! Down you were prodded by the Devil with a three-pronged fork and kept there for all eternity! Good God! I nearly fainted with fear. I remember I did cry out in sheer terror; but then I realised that to cry out in church might be one of the very sins that would certainly send me to Hell! So I pulled myself together.

Then a great hope came to me in the thought that, after all, one was only burnt in Hell if one were *bad*. So, thought I, " By gosh, I'll be good! " But then the most terrible fact of all came out when our spiritual adviser assured us that from the time before we were born it was written in the Book of God and foreordained whether we would burn in Hell or escape it! Even as a bairn I thought this rather discouraging. There didn't seem much point in trying to be good.

That night at bedtime I was the most scared wee fellow that the world ever contained. With tears I appealed to my mother for some ray of hope and comfort. But she, poor woman, had had the reality of Hell dinned into her all her life and could only hug me and hope that we were both on the list of the " chosen of God." It was a small crumb but I grasped it. What else was there for a wee fellow to do?

Looking back on my earliest years I can truthfully say that Hell and the fear of it was never far from our minds and even on those few occasions when we dipped into some innocent frolic, Hell hung in the near background like a skeleton at a feast.

From church-going friends I am given to understand that Hell nowadays is rather disowned by the clergy—that, in fact, they are rather ashamed of the old institution and are inclined to the use of plausible sophistries calculated to reconcile the veritable thing Hell was in the view of the clergy of forty years ago with the allegorical thing into which it has now degenerated in the ecclesiastical mind.

Well, well! Other days other ways. But indeed I have difficulty in thinking kindly of the old Hell and those who preached it.

Notwithstanding the inescapibility of Hell for those predestined to it, our moral mentors—most illogically, I thought—were ever urging all of us to " good " actions for the propitiation of the Deity, and surely none was more puzzling than in regard to our conduct on the Sabbath!

To seek to edify your mind on that day by reading Shakespeare or Scott was one of the unforgiveable sins; but you were free to debase it in uncharitable gossip with your neighbour to your heart's content!

It was permissible to cut tobacco with a knife on Sunday, but not on any account might you cut a string or a stick, or even the vegetables for the broth!

You might wash your face on the Lord's day; indeed you were expected to; but you were heading

straight for perdition if you shaved it! or cut your
nails!

If your boots were left unbrushed on the Satur-
day night, then unbrushed they must remain over
Sunday if you wanted to escape eternal punishment! But you might brush your beard without
risk.

There was no sin in taking the horses to the
water to drink; but your neighbours shuddered
for you soul if you reversed the process by taking
the water from the pond to the horses! That was
a very subtle one!

You daren't peel the potatoes on Sunday before
cooking them; but, once boiled, they could be
peeled with impunity!

Altogether, there was a fine, hair-splitting dis-
crimination between the things you might and
might not do on the first day of the week, that was
always puzzling to myself; and no amount of Wee
MacGreegor inquisitiveness in the way of " Whit
wey, Ma? " ever shed much light on " The reason
o' the cause an' the wherefore o' the why."

CHAPTER XX

The Schoolie — Moloch of Learning — Corochans — Going Barefeet.

IF there is one class of fellow-mortals that I have more sympathy for than another on those bonnie summer mornings, it is the scholars at a country school when the harsh jangle of the bell so ruthlessly calls them from the enchantment that lies without, to the drab tasks that lie within the walls of the school-room. Poor, unwilling sacrifices on the altar of the Moloch of Learning!

In the city it is not so bad; from drab street to drabber class-room is merely a matter of degree of misery. But in the country. . . . ! To have to file into that depressing atmosphere of square roots, G.C.M.'s and " goes-into's," when the sun is shining gloriously and out-of-door allurements are strong. . . . !

There is the wood with its carpet of wild flowers; there are the nests so cunningly hidden in the banks and bushes of the burnside. And the trout . . . ! O! *mo thruaighe!* that the hard necessity of acquiring book-learning should tear us from the Nature's Academy that is there!

We used to spend up till the very last minute in climbing trees, in guddling for trout, in exploring—until the clanging of that thrice-cursèd bell. And if we didn't quite jump to the call, who that was ever a boy can blame us! In any case we expiated the crime of being late by a stolid acceptance of the pandies the old dominie conscientiously administered—for we had had our *quid pro quo*.

The nests of the Blackie and the Mavy and the Binkie (chaffinch) and the *Buidheag* (yellowhammer) were fairly common, but there was a special thrill in the finding of a Jennie Wren's nursery with its wee doorie that only the hand of the littlest lassie could get into to count the eggs. Then there was the rarer nest of the " Needlack " that was built of withered grass in a hole in the ground. There was a pair of perky Robins that built for three successive years in a discarded kettle that lay in the wood. . . .

I wonder if the boys at the old school still dig for *Corochans?* Or if they know what *Corochans* are? They are little lumps or nodules that grow on the roots of a certain purple-flowered vetch. When we came on a bed of them we carefully pulled away the grass, and then with our knives dug down into the earth until we got to the much prized *corochan* that was believed to have the special virtue of imparting " strength," and what boy does not want to be strong?

One *corochan* would keep a boy chewing for an hour, but the great thing was to save up until you had a dozen or so to pop into your mouth at once.

That was a bon-bon de luxe. Or, alternatively, it had a considerable barter value in the way of marbles, transfers, knives and skeany strings.

I am kind of ashamed to confess that I never had the moral courage to " slip " the school; not indeed because of any particular diligence in learning; it was rather because of a shrewd antici-patory instinct in regard to the parental chastise-ment which would follow—or pained reproach which was even worse. But how I envied those devil-may-care companions who had the pluck to " slip " for a day or two of stolen freedom! One such I can think of has for many years been an ornament in the County Constabulary. On the principle that a clever poacher makes the best gamekeeper he should be just about the most efficient member of the " force," for verily that Bobby as a boy was the impish limit. But I hope he is not another example of that numerous class of people who allow the years to blot out the recollection of their own boyish pranks; and that when he is called upon to deal with youthful delinquents a memory of the boy that once he was will cause him to temper justice with mercy.

It may be a delusion of the memory but, looking back, it does seem that in those years the winters were more decidedly seasons of frost and snow, and the summers of warmth and sunshine than they are now. In any case it was an unwritten rule amongst the school-boys that boots were discarded on May-day, and only brought into commission

again when the first snow and frost of winter compelled that literally cramping step. Should May-
day prove exceptionally cold, parental authority
might decree that boots must still be worn, but in
that event convention and youthful *esprit-de-corps*
demanded they should travel no farther than the
nut-wood where they were removed and hidden in
rabbit-holes till evening when it was deemed
prudent to put them on again on the homeward
way.

Going " barefeet " without parental leave was
an offence punishable by the master; but, whether
to our credit or discredit, the crime was rarely
punished because it was rarely confessed. Probably
we felt there was punishment enough in the cuts
and sores on tender soles and toes that accompanied the first few days of pedal freedom!   But
by the end of a fortnight a sort of leather sole
would develop that was an effective protection
against thorn-stabs and sharp gravel, and we could
run with the swiftness and freedom of nature until

> " the snaw it stopped the herdin' an' the
>   winter broch him dool,
> When in spite o' hacks and chilblains
>   he was shod again for school."

CHAPTER XXI

A Garden Sweet and Fair—A Bobby and a Gentleman.

WRITING of the Bobby with the lurid boyhood reminds me of another arm of the law; and he was gifted with wisdom.

On our way to school we passed by the side of a garden; and such a garden! It had trees laden with apples and pears and plums; there were luscious strawberries, tart gooseberries and fat green peas; Nyum, nyum! Between us and these there was only a stone wall with black and red-currant bushes growing against its inner side and over the top, whose fruit just hung to our hands. At home and in school we were duly instructed in the virtue of strict honesty and had ingrained in us a highly realistic conception of the torture by fire that was the ultimate reward of thieving. But, I ask you. . . .?

Anyhow, occasionally even the dread of a future roasting proved ineffectual as a deterrent. Besides we soothed our consciences with the sophistry that even if we did resist the temptation, the chances were that most of that fruit would be left to rot where it had ripened!

The owner of the garden was an old lady, who,

during the last thirty years of a life-span of ninety-nine spent most of her days sitting in rigid state in an arm-chair in the drawing-room. I set eyes on her only once, and the sight of her in bustled skirt, lace shawl and long, white ringleted hair and leaning on a gold-topped staff, remains in my memory as the picture of a being from another age—almost from another planet.

Experience soon taught us that the swiftest pace of the middle-aged maid who valeted the old lady was not quite up to the speed of the slowest of our group, and safe in that knowledge we would continue guzzling till the very last moment—till, in fact, we heard the click of the garden gate.

I have often wondered about that click. She could have opened the gate quietly—but she never did. Why? I think kindly of that woman. . . .!

One evening we were well ensconced among the gooseberry bushes and the rows of peas. The gate clicked. We rose leisurely to scamper off in the usual way; and just then we got the shock! Later we learned that the usual maid had gone for a holiday, but all we saw at the time was an athletic lassie of twenty sprinting straight for us! We stood not on the order of our going. Over the wall and up the path by the side of the corn-field we streaked with Atlanta in hot pursuit. Alas, we had no Hippomenesian golden apples to tempt her curiosity or to check her speed, and it was only a matter of moments till she had " Bumbee " by the pleats of his kilt. Poor Bumbee! That

was the fright of his life. Sudden death was the
least that would happen if he didn't tell her
straight off the name of every raider. Bumbee
had no wish to die just yet—he was only nine and
in robust health—so who can blame him if he spat
out the names at the double? And he took no
chances, for he gave " full measure, pressed down
and running over " by including in the list the
names of some unfortunates who were not there
that evening! For this " plus " information the
wretched Bumbee was made to pay in nasal blood
later on; but that is another story. . . .

There was a loud rap at the school door next
forenoon. The dominie came back with a grave
face and our hearts sunk lower than our boots
when he called our names, ordered us to " take the
floor " and then informed us that in the lobby
there was " a gentleman " wishing to see us.

I shall not forget that first interview with a
policeman if I live to be as old as the owner of
the garden. He was more solemn than a minister,
and so concerned at our plight!!!

" I am awfully sorry, boys," said he, in a slow,
kind voice that nearly made us cry, " but of course
I cannot help it. Jile is the only thing for thieving." (pause). "And the beds there are just
boards! " . . . " and it will be nothing but bread
and water three times a day for a fortnight!!—
and not much of that!! " After a final pause to
allow the awful horrors sink well into our sickened
souls he walked slowly to the door. The younger

ones were now blubbering, and the older ones were just holding on.

Then he came back. "Maybe," said he—allowing just a shade of hope creep into his voice— "Mind, I cannot promise, but maybe if I could see the Sheriff and tell him that you are really a nice lot of boys and that you are awfully sorry, and that you promise not to steal from Miss M's garden again, he might let you off. Will you promise me that?"

Promise? . . . like a shot we did, and as with one voice!

"Mind you," cautioned this wise old man, "I cannot promise that the Sheriff will let you off, but I will do the best I can for you—but it will be two or three weeks before you can be sure!"

Needless to say that was the last we heard of the matter, and we never went near that garden again —at least not until that policeman retired.

Many times have I thought since then how literally true was the dominie's intimation to us on that memorable morning; "a gentleman" indeed had come to see us.

CHAPTER XXII

School Fights.

On the whole, we were a friendly lot at the old school, but occasionally something would occur that demanded the arbitrament on arms—or fisticuffs. No doubt a mother of the namby pamby kind, then as now, would be horrified to think that her dear wee Johnnie might come in for rough treatment at the hands of the " rude, bad boys " ; but the fact remains that in the roughish, hardy training that is the lot of a lad at the average country school, there is much that is invaluable to him in after life.

Fights were mainly of three varieties. First there was the fight which the bigger boys " commanded " between two juniors. The seniors would have a difference of opinion as to whether little Jimmac could beat wee Alickie, and to settle the point nothing would do but that the two juniors—who might be the greatest of friends—must doff caps and jackets and set-to to pummel each other. There was no rancour at all in such encounters. A bleeding nose on either side usually sufficed to resolve the doubt and the interrupted friendship was immediately resumed.

Then there was the fight arising from lost tempers and heated passions. These were more serious affairs and usually resulted in a good deal of blood—bad and otherwise.

But the most serious type of fight was the one that had a moral background. Anything in the nature of bullying was by common accord condemned. Any boy who ill-treated one obviously younger and weaker than himself would be promptly advised to " chuck it "—and, if he disregarded the advice, things were likely to happen pretty quickly. That was the origin of the greatest fight at our school in my time.

We were having an exciting game of shinty in the minutes just before the two-o'clock bell. The centre-forward on one side happened to be one of a family that had for years provided a school-bully. He was hated, yet feared by all. So far no one had dared question his authority. On this occasion, to the bully's chagrin, a timid little " back " but an adept with the caman, had twice prevented his scoring a hail. When this happened still a third time, the bully " lost his rag " and proceeded to make a most cowardly attack on poor wee Roddie. The game stopped. We were horrified. Then, before the rest of us could pick up courage to intervene, a voice came from the most unexpected quarter.

" Chuck that, Sparks! " commanded Dinker in a tone we had never heard from him before. Sparks was so flabbergasted at being thus addressed that he actually did " chuck it " so far as Roddie was concerned. Dinker was the quietest, most modest boy in the whole school, and nearly a year younger than Sparks. He had no particular gift for learning, but he had a gift for sympathy and friendship, and a comical sort of humorous twist of a smile and a turn for harmless mischief that made him a prime favourite amongst both boys and girls. But never once had Dinker been in a fight; and that he should be the one to pull him up was as astonishing to Sparks as it must have been to King Solomon if one of his meanest slaves had dared him to marry another wife! !

Outraged dignity shone in Spark's eye when at last he recovered from the shock, and he was on the point of transferring his attack from Roddie to Dinker when the bell rang.

There was a tense atmosphere in school that afternoon. Like a flash the news went round that Dinker had " cheeked " Sparks! Sparks glowered surreptitiously at the mutineer and spluttered threats of four o'clock annihilation. Dinker said nothing; he didn't even smile. If he regretted what he had done he never let on. The great question was, would he fight?—or would he just take what was coming to him? To us the one alternative was as unthinkable as the other.

But by a quarter to four Dinker gave us the second thrill of that day when he calmly announced he would fight.

The old dominie must have wondered why the playground cleared so quickly that autumn afternoon. The scholars en masse repaired to the green in the Church Woodie—the recognised arena for the big fights. A ring of excited juvenile humanity was quickly formed. Sparks, true to his name, still issued threats of direst punishment. Dinker, still silent, with set face, handed cap and jacket to his young brother.

That fight was an epic. Smarting from a sense of insulted majesty, Sparks (who, to do him justice, was a real soldier), went for Dinker like a fury. No other boy I have known would have stood up against that onslaught. But Dinker stood up to it and, gradually, though the sweat and blood that soon profusely adorned his countenance, the old comical twist of a smile became discernible—but it had a grim shade in it.

From defence, Dinker went to attack. And such an attack! For good hard hitting, skill and sheer dour, dogged pluck, I have never seen his equal. Sparks fought gamely, but within half-an-hour his nose was battered to pulp, his two eyes were closed, three front teeth had gone and altogether what had been his face presented literally the bloodiest mess it is possible to imagine. Twice did Dinker pause to inquire of the other if he had had enough, and it was not until the third time, when Sparks was at last thoroughly beaten and demoralised, that the answer was in the affirmative.

It was an impressive scene; we had witnessed the

H

deposition of a tyrannical king. There was whole-hearted joy amongst boys and girls alike. But Dinker, with characteristic modesty, never made any reference to his one and only fight.

CHAPTER XXIII

Sgadan's Strategy.

PRACTICAL joking may not be a very elegant form of wit; indeed there is no fun in it at all when carried to excess and I'm not saying but some of the pranks the previous generation used to play on each other went over the score in that direction. On the other hand, when kept within bounds there was a lot of laughter and no real harm done. The victim might be the butt of the ceilidh or the school for the time being, but it was always open to him to retaliate; and the urge to do so had a fine sharpening effect on the wits.

On the whole we rather liked Calum Mòr, but, unfortunately for us, his idea of a grand practical joke was to steal our clothes while we were bathing, during the play-hour, in a pool of the river that ran through his croft. There was a fringe of alder bushes which afforded him cover in his stealthy raids and the first thing we would hear would be a whoop of delight from Calum as he ran off with all the kilts and shirts and corduroy trousers he could hurriedly grab—for well he knew from experience that he must not wait long within range

115

of the fusillade of stones with which we pelted him—if only we could spot him in time!

It is true our predicament was not without one streak of comfort. When Calum stole our clothes we had a very sound excuse for not going to school in the afternoon. Indeed I'm not saying but some of us would never blink an eye when, as a reason for absence we tendered to the dominie the tale of Calum's wickedness on occasions when poor Calum was quite innocent. But that was a risky expedient which sometimes culminated in acute physical discomfort!

One summer, though, Calum was more than usually successful with his "joke." We were getting fed-up with him. There is nothing more disconcertingly humiliating for a boy than to be denuded of his conventional covering in broad daylight. The indignities we suffered in having, in our natal state, to implore Calum to return our garments were more than we could be expected to continue to bear.

It was the "*Sgadan's*" (Herring's) fertile brain that saw the way to revenge. Sgadan had observed Calum's tactics closely. He always approached from the west, grabbed the booty off the bank and instead of turning back, carried on eastwards by a little path than ran parallel to the river's edge and close to the pool which was so deep and swirling that we never bathed in it. No doubt, Calum's reason for choosing this line of retreat was the fact that a big alder bush grew

between it and our pool so that it afforded him a
partial protection from our " fire." But there was
a monotony about the plan that for ever rules
Calum out of the category of great strategists—and
incidentally shows Sgadan as a bright and shining
light. For, not only did our hero see in the
enemy's tactics the opportunity for his overthrow
but, with a fine dramatic instinct he never divulged
his plan till our eyes beheld its greatness. We
were splashing about in our pool one day when
Sgadan let out the usual warning yell of " clothes."
He must have been sharply on the look-out that
day for Calum had only time to snatch a *ciotag*
(rag) or two before a barrage of stones was getting
him right and left! Off he set as hard as he could
leg it along the usual path. Then all of a sudden
he made the finest *car a mhuiltean* (somersault)
ever you saw right into the *Poll-grannda* (nasty
pool).

As we ran towards the black pool Sgadan yelled
a warning—" Ware! grass-snares! " We grasped
the situation just in time to prevent some of ourselves sharing Calum's unfortunate fate. Sgadan,
the evening before, had knotted a series of handfuls of the long tough grass so that they formed
" snares " across the path; and it was one of these
that had given his *conge* to Calum in his more
than usually precipitate flight.

Believe me, we drove a hard bargain with our
tormentor in regard to future immunity before we
hauled him out of the *Poll-grannda*! And the

minor tragedy of poor wee Davock's kilt—which
Calum had carried with him into the pool, and
which was never recovered—was forgotten in the
joy of victory—and another half-holiday!

CHAPTER XXIV

Hector and Diamond—Curing a Jibber.

WHEN Donull Og used to criticise his neighbour Rory for failing to keep his rather high-flying wife in proper subjection, his own wife Eilidh would slyly retort: *"Tha sin gle mhath, a Dhonuill, ach ceannsaichidh a h-uile fear an droch bhean ach a' fear aig am bi'i!"*—"That is all very well, Donald, but every man can discipline the bad wife but the man who has got her."

And this is as true of horses as it is of wives. It's all very well to criticise the other man's inept handling, but it must be a right awkward predicament to be landed with either a wicked horse or wife.

Take a kicker, for instance—and, by the way, it is interesting to note that horses afflicted with this particular vice are, almost without exception, of the female sex! A kicking mare is a real problem. She may be going along as meekly as a lamb the one moment, and the next it would seem that all the seven devils that are usually associated with the pig have got possession of her, for she proceeds with fiendish venom to kick your good cart to smithereens. It takes a really philosophic driver to stand that sort of thing with unruffled temper.

And look at the jibber, that coaxing or cursing or caning will not induce to move forward one step! I never see a jibber but I remember that ploy we played on *Eachann Bodhar* (Deaf Hector) and his horse, Diamond, many years ago.

Eachann used to go with his horse and cart to Dingwall once a fortnight or so. On the way home, when they came to the end of the level road and turned to face the half-mile brae, it was Diamond's invariable habit to stolidly refuse to advance another yard, for maybe an hour or more, that must have felt like a day to the impatient Eachann. Eachann might apply the whip and some shocking language as forcibly as he liked (and he did!), but Diamond would not budge. After ten minutes of this forceful but futile persuasion, Eachann would give it up as a bad job, and, sitting on a board that rested on the two sides of the cart just forward of the wheels, would proceed to fill the old clay pipe and suck such comfort as he could from it until at long last it suited Diamond's pleasure to resume the homeward way. This was a most humiliating wait for the irascible Eachann, and we youngsters never failed to exhibit our fiendish glee at his dilemma, until our bright leader conceived and executed a plan which robbed us for ever of that diversion.

The plot was carefully laid. One evening we hid behind the dyke at the corner where we knew that Eachann and Diamond would soon arrive. They duly came. Eachann turned Diamond to

face the hill.   As per usual, Diamond stopped,
and Eachann as per usual, stooped forward in the
cart and belaboured the refractory one with the
usual admixture of whip and tongue, with the
usual result.   Then he gave it up and sat down
on the board to get the pipe agoing.   It was at
that moment the Bright One crept in close behind
the cart, carrying in his hand an enormous " dag "
that a soldier-uncle had brought home from the
Crimea.   This pistol had a strong and capacious
barrel that we had charged to near the mouth with
black blasting powder (taken from the quarrymen's
bothy, I'm afraid) and packed in with a wad com-
posed of a compressed page of a newspaper.

The explosion, right at Diamond's heels, was
as terrific as it was unexpected.   Diamond gave
one forward spring and then set off up the brae
at a gallop which never slackened till he reached
home.   At the first spring Eachan lost his balance
and fell backwards heels-over-head into the bottom
of the cart, where he was quite safe, though rattled
like a pea in a pail; and the one glance we got of
his face as Diamond careered along showed on it
the most amazed surprise you ever saw!

Never once in after years did Diamond try his
old trick at the bottom of the brae; and at that
Eachann was delighted.   But the funniest part of
the story is that, what between his deafness and
the suddenness of the whole affair, he never knew
exactly " what came at " Diamond on that memorable day—and we were too afraid to tell.

CHAPTER XXV

Caol an Fhuaim or Channel of the Roaring Waters.

Away back over a century ago, the people of a township on one of the main islands of the Hebrides were evicted by the Tacksman from the little crofts which had been theirs and their fore-bears for generations.

We need not enter into the rights or wrongs of the case; maybe there were faults on both sides. But it was with sore hearts the people packed up their little belongings, stowed them in boats and flitted them over the Sound to the uninhabited island which was to be their future home. It was late autumn. They expected a winter of priva-tion, for their stores were meagre; but the storms which came that winter were unusually severe and protracted; so that, to this day on the island it is spoken of as " the wild winter of the year of the flitting."

The surface of their new island was mainly rock and rough grazing. True, there was a belt of good *machair* land fringing the bay, round the sides of which they built the rude stone-and-turf dwellings which afforded but indifferent shelter from the storms that every now and then raged across the island and lashed the surrounding sea to fury. But it would be next September before the *machair* could be made to yield a harvest that would give them bread, and provide fodder for the few head of cattle they had managed to take with them— and the assurance of a good meal in September is poor comfort to a hungry belly the previous April! Yet manure, cultivate and sow the *machair* they must if they were to survive another winter. So they cut seaware and carried it in creels to fertilise the land. Then they turned the earth with the *cas-chrom,* sowed with care the few pecks of seed-grain and left the rest to the Almighty.

On a day that April, half-a-dozen of the young men were cutting seaware. As the tide receded they followed up with their *corrans,* cutting the newly exposed ware and carrying it to safety out-with the reach of high tide. From there, in creels it was carried by the girls to the *machair.* It was heavy work and demanded much energetic attention from all; but they were young and irresponsible enough to enjoy a little diversion each time the lassies returned to the *cladach* with empty creels for another load. Then there was some of that banter and laughter which has ever been the way with young folks, and not even the privations incidental to existence on their new island could quite smother its expression that spring day.

Late in the afternoon didn't *Mairi,* the daughter of Donald Morrison, come to the *cladach* in the capacity of nurse to her baby brother, Colin. To guard against the bairn injuring its tender limbs on the stony beach, Mairi rolled him in blankets, and for extra safety laid him in a tub which was sometimes used for containing whelks and cockles or other shell-fish, and which now stood well clear of the tide. The child thus safely disposed of, Mairi joined in the fun with the others.

In certain circumstances time has a way of flying. It flew now with Mairi and her companions. Suddenly they realised that it was almost dark and that the tide had " made " rapidly!—The bairn . . . ! Swiftly they ran over the intervening rocks to where the child had been left in the tub—but, to their horror no trace of child or tub could be seen. Distractedly they ran, this way and that, shouting and scanning, but to no avail. . . .

It was when the panic was at its height that Angus *Og*—a lad wise for his years—said in that quiet compelling way of his: " This is not the time for useless wailing. This is a case for *Calum Glic* " (Wise Malcolm). And like the wind he set off for the earthen hut which was Calum's dwelling.

" Calum," gasped Angus, " Donald Morrison's bairn is carried off with the tide. He was in the cockle-tub at the *cladach* and we forgot about him! "

Calum—a man of uncanny insight and little speech—except on occasion when he could be eloquent enough—went without a word to the shore.

There the jollity of but an hour before had changed into the gloom of dread. Calum demanded information—exact information—as to the spot where the tub had stood. Did it contain any cockles? or was it just weighted with the child?——The wind?—its strength—when did it change? He asked for the information jerkily, but with command in his voice. The youths gave him to the best of their recollection.

Then Calum appeared for some minutes to go into a trance. He stared at the stars and could be heard muttering. Well the young folks knew his problem. He was trying to read the riddle of the tides, making due allowance for the effect of varying winds. Round to the East of their new island, in the channel which separated it from the neighbouring land there is the rather rare phenomenon, contending tides. There, twice daily, the tide from the Minch rushes westwards while the tide from the Atlantic rushes eastwards, both with the speed of a fast river. They meet in mid channel and wild is the resulting commotion. That channel is known locally as *Caol-an-fhuaim* (The Channel of the Noisy Waters). That night the tub containing Donald Morrison's youngest born would be wafted gently by the south-west wind that blew an hour ago, until it got caught in the swift flow of the current from the Minch. Then nothing could save it from being engulfed in the dreaded waters of *Caol-an-fhuaim*. True, the wind had changed and now blew freshly from the west; but no! no! Not even the wisdom and skill of *Calum Glic* could give them a glint of hope!

Calum was now coming out of his trance. He was quite calm, but under great strain. Then he thundered in a voice that made the lads jump to obey, " Put out the big boat."

In a trice the boat was ready.

" *Athainne!* (A Torch) " was Calum's next command; and in a twinkling black peats with one glowing end were brought from the big fire they had kindled at mid-day in the shelter of a rock. They also put some unkindled peats in the boat.

Four men went to the oars. Each of other four held in his hand, by the cold end, a peat with lighted end to the wind so that it glowed, and a considerable halo of light shone on the waters round the boat.

" Steer on that blue star to the south of east," Calum commanded.

For an hour they pulled, with never a word spoken except for an occasional brief command from Calum. Right out they went over the dark and now stormy waters of the Minch. As one peat nearly burnt itself out another was set to its glow till it also took fire; and so the torch-light was continuous. But the wind was growing stronger. Peat after peat got more quickly finished.

" Dip them in the sea " ordered Calum. This was done, and the damped peat lasted a little longer. But soon even this plan would not suffice.

The peats were nearly finished. . . . Soon they would be in darkness and without a vestige of hope. . . .

But Calum, for the past few minutes had been keenly scanning the sea. His eyes, though old, seemed to cut into the darkness. Suddenly, and with the first touch of emotion his voice had shown, he shouted to Angus *Og* who was holding the last glowing ember of the last peat in fingers that were burning with the heat of it: "*Tog suas an t-athainne!*" (Lift up the torch!).

Up went the torch to the full stretch of Angus *Og's* arm, and there, within the halo cast by the burning peat, was the cockle-tub, smoothly riding the waves! And inside it, with uplifted arms and cherubic smile, the newly awakened child of Donald Morrison.

Then, in the middle of the marvel of it Calum removed the bonnet from his white head that shone in the light of the peat and reverently thanked his Maker for the guidance He had vouchsafed to His unworthy servant.

CHAPTER XXVI

The Trysting Place.

No, this is not a love story. It's a story of another sort of trysting place altogether, and of a shepherd and his dog connected therewith, and some other things.

As you leave the town of Inverness and travel up by the Great North Road you pass through a country of rare beauty and interest. Inverness itself is definitely left behind when you rumble over the narrow bridge that spans the Caledonian Canal. A new modern bridge is now in course of erection. To the left of the road the ground rises steeply to Clachnaharry, a rocky height from which, in the old days watch was kept against the approach of enemies.

Close by the road on the right, the Beauly Firth lies like a burnished sword, bending and sharpening to a point that stabs the heart of the hills. Across the Firth lies the Black Isle. The name does it a rank injustice, for its wide fringes round the shores of the Beauly and Cromarty Firths present a pleasing picture of green trees and fertile, well-tilled farms.

In the far distance Ben Wyvis rears its solemn massive bulk bathing in the sunlight, but with a

128

few spots of snow still showing in its deeper
corries.   Or it may be that you can only catch a
shadowy glimpse of the Ben itself as the clouds
and mist scud across, or enshroud it in calm white
mystery.   But whatever its guise, and whether
under summer's sun or winter's snow, it is one of
those sublime things in nature which never fails
to stir the finer emotions of the human mind.

Some four miles from Inverness is Bunchrew
with its narrow belt of fertile fields and its lovely
woods where Neil Munro's *Beachdair* slept in the
cave by the side of the burn and guddled for trout
for his breakfast.

Another few miles and you pass the old Bog
Roy Inn where in bygone days the smugglers outwitted the gaugers.   The gaugers had captured a
cask of whisky in a smugglers' bothy nearby, and
had it taken into a room in the Inn pending its
removal to Inverness.   To make doubly sure of
its safety (they had been outwitted before) two
gaugers sat on top of the cask while a third walked
back to Inverness for a horse and cart.   But the
smugglers, reluctant to part with the potent fruit
of their labour (and helped by the hints of a
friendly servant-lassie) quietly entered a room immediately below the one in which the cask and
the gaugers sat, placed another cask " plumb
below " and bored a hole with an augur through
the floor and cask above.   The spirit obeyed the
ordinary law of gravity, and when the horse and
cart, etc., arrived from Inverness the gaugers soon

I

discovered to their chagrin that their prize now consisted of an empty cask!

Soon you are passing through the Lovat country and the rich alluvial lands that once belonged to the Monastery. You cross the river Beauly by the bridge of that name—there is always a chance of seeing a salmon leap in the pool below—and then turn sharply to the right for the village. On the left, about two miles distant, and just discernible over a wealth of tree-tops stands Beaufort Castle, the ancestral home of the Lovat family, and nearby there are the ruins of Castle Dounie, closely associated with many stirring episodes in Scottish history.

The village of Beauly itself, with its quaint wide square, its shops and trim villas and its ruins of the Old Priory makes a pleasant and restful picture. It is true that now-a-days many buses pass through the village—indeed they stop there for a few minutes—but, as they are smoothly designed and tastefully coloured buses, and as their passengers are usually quiet and reflective people, even these modern transport vehicles do not seem out of place in this charming Highland hamlet.

Still another mile further north and the road for some two hundred yards winds gracefully up a brae. At the top of the brae a new picture is, as it were, thrown on the screen. You are now on an old raised beach as flat as a table for two miles in front and for half a mile on either side. The soil is light and shingly and there is a profusion of whin and broom which—if it happens to be June or July—looks like a carpet of gold.

There is plenty of variety dimly discernible in the far distance, and I should like to carry you with me to the farther north where there is breath-catching beauty round every bend of the road. But for the present at least we can go no farther, for we have arrived at our Trysting Place—the Muir-of-Ord.

The Muir-of-Ord is now a golf course—shade of Corrychoillie! (a noted worthy of the Market). It that was once the Falkirk Tryst of the north! Here in the old days, once every month, met farmers and flockmasters, crofters and shepherds, bringing with them thousands of sheep and hundreds of cattle for the purpose of selling to each other and to the farmers and dealers and drovers that came from the south.

As a small boy I attended the Market for the first time well over forty years ago. Even then it was past its best for the Auction Mart had carried its invasion to the north some years previously. But there was still a great gathering of men and dogs and beasts, and that first day stands out a landmark in the memory.

There were fair-haired Scandinavians from the plains of Caithness with never a word of Gaelic in their heads; they and their beasts had been on the road for ten days. Then there were the big flock-masters from Ross-shire and Sutherland, of whom not a few were the descendants of Border men who had migrated north some decades previously, and in conclave with impecunious proprietors, appropriated extensive grazings that had previously belonged to the native peasantry. And there were big, bearded, picturesque men from Skye and the Hebrides with their equally picturesque Highland cattle whose horns spanned six feet and more. There were also hundreds of small farmers and crofters from far and near. Men from north and south of the Border were there in plenty, mostly with clean or partly-shaven faces, coloured by a sun-cum-whisky admixture to various tints of red and brown.

No two men were dressed alike; each man seemed to have a distinctive garb of his own. One gentleman I particularly noticed wore elastic-sided boots, trousers of the shepherd tartan pattern, a blue-green coat with tails, a flaming red gravat and a tall, tapered flat-topped hat; and all over, there vas a picturesque display of colour and individuality in dress and character that is woefully lacking at the ringside of the modern auction mart.

And what a confusion of sheep and cattle and dogs and shepherds and shouting! To the uninitiated it seemed that never could order come out of that chaos. But order did come eventually; each lot was stanced and the battle of buying and selling began. It was a hard school and it was intensely interesting to watch and listen to the experts at work. With what withering scorn

Alastair Breac could point out the defects in a lot of beasts he wanted to buy! and then the convincing manner in which he revealed to prospective purchasers the admirable qualities of that same lot later in the day when he wanted to sell them! A day at the Muir was a liberal lesson in tact, diplomacy, guile and a hundred other arts useful to existence in this hard world! There every man had better have a shrewd idea of the value of what he wanted to sell or buy, and he required to have the courage of his convictions; for indeed the Market was no place for fools. One wonders how the rising generation of farmers would fare in a battle of wits with Alastair Breac and his kind. Badly, I fear, for open, competitive bidding and the weigh-bridge of the auction mart have deprived them of the opportunity of exercising their personal skill and judgment.

As lots changed ownership, so did wads of notes —or, better still, solid golden sovereigns—and soon the refreshment tent was doing a roaring trade. The bar-tender's job was simple in those days for he had practically one drink to serve—the wine of the country, at 4d. per half gill, and nobody thought of taking a smaller measure than that at a time. They were hard drinkers then, and could carry an amazing quantity with impunity, or at any rate without detriment to their bargaining acumen.

It was to this Market that Bob Cairns came every autumn in charge of his master's ewes. Bob

was shepherd on an outlying hirsel of a farm situ-
ated some fifteen miles from the Muir. He was
one of those Border shepherds who moved north
with the cheviot sheep, and these men were in a
class by themselves at that time. They were
artists in their profession and the main object in
their lives was to present to their employers when
Market day arrived the finest lot of sheep that hard
work and care and skill could possibly produce.
Rivalry in the matter of prices was keen, and the
shepherd took a keener pride than his master in
overtaking or beating a neighbouring lot in the
Market.

(It is but fair to interject here that that spirit
and tradition are still to be met with amongst
that very superior class of men, and that the
natives of the north have not been slow in learning
the craft; so that now men with names like
Sutherland or MacKay may hold their own with
Scotts, or Waughs or Armstrongs).

But Bob's strongest point was his training of
dogs. He had a gift for that. No floggings nor
senseless shouting were part of Bob's method, but
that quiet voice, even temper, gentle but firm
reproof and judicious encouragement—in fact it
was as one gentleman to another; and the result
was superb, for Bob and his dogs were noted over
a wide district.

One of the very best dogs he ever had was Risp,
a beautiful black collie with a white ruff and
white-tipped nose and tail. Risp was reputed to

be able to do anything but speak. To those who have witnessed a sheep-dog trial, the collie's almost incredible intelligence and sagacity are known. The dogs at those trials have been specially trained to become expert in controlling a certain limited number of "situations," but the problems which confront the ordinary shepherd's working dog in the course of a heavy day—problems demanding instant solution—are innumerable; and Risp was master of his calling. Moreover—what is rather rare in a good working dog—he would frolic with the bairns like a puppy. He and Bob Junior, four years old, and second youngest of a family of ten, were boon companions in fun when Risp had an hour to spare.

When Mrs Cairns' tenth child arrived on the scene, wee Bobbie and Risp felt rather uncomfortable about it, and gave that squalling youngster a wide berth. But soon he was the unconscious cause of great grief to both.

A sort of double-faced problem confronted Bob Cairns; the baby had to be baptised and he (Bob) had to go to the Muir-of-Ord Market. One might think that that problem shouldn't present any great difficulty; but it did, and it's just as well to make the confession here. Bob had one weakness —if indeed it amounted to that. Anyhow, like many a good shepherd living a lonely hard-working life in a remote glen he rejoiced to meet his fellows, and the Market was his one opportunity. There the pent-up austerity of a long year would be effectively drowned in the social bowl. There would be a few glorious hours of "kindled wit and waukened lair" and utterly happy companionship with half a dozen good fellows whom he hadn't seen, and wouldn't see again, for twelve long months; and they would make a night of it—and in short they would have a glorious spree. That had happened to Bob with unfailing regularity—once a year—and who dare say, in all the circumstances, that it did not do him a lot of good?

But the new minister was very strict in the administration of the baptismal sacrament, and he, unfortunately, late on the night of the previous Market had come across Bob and two friends lying in the bottom of a peat hag—fortunately a dry one—into which they had stumbled, singing at the top of their voices with the enthusiasm that is spirituously inspired, each with a bottle in his hand and another in his pocket. Nor did the advent of the minister appreciably damp their enthusiasm for they had attained victory over the ills of life.

His Reverence lacked that sympathetic understanding which Bob's wife displayed on these occasions; he was shocked and angry.

As the date of the Market drew near, therefore, Bob became uneasy in his mind at the thought of the visit to the manse. He looked so glum at breakfast one morning that his wife remarked in her cheeriest voice, "What's the matter with you this morning, Bob? You haven't eaten half your

porridge!—and your face is no' just beaming! "
and then in that sympathetic, understanding way
she had she added, " It's no' the minister and the
baptism that's bothering you, is it? "

" You've struck it first time, Meg," said Bob in
a rueful tone, " that's just what is bothering me."

" Bob! " said Meg, coming over to her husband's
chair and placing a sympathetic hand on his head,
" You shouldn't let that bother you, lad. You
have nothing to be ashamed of, and surely Mr
MacLeod must know by this time what sort of man
Bob Cairns really is."

Bob caught her hand in a grip that hurt. " It's
just like you to say that, Meg," he replied, " but
you see Mr MacLeod does not look at me with
your eyes; and I'll admit that that night he found
Davie Scott and Jock Elliot and myself singing and
drinking in the peat-hag, we were pretty bad.
Indeed I can't mind much of what happened but
I'm sure that Davie offered him a dram and I
think I wanted to argue with him about religion!
Oh! he was very angry, and there was no fun in
him at all; and I didn't like his look when I met
him in Garvalt last month! "

" Never mind, Bob," consoled his wife, " It's
your only day off in the year, and he might have
more sense than to take any notice; and besides,"
she added, with a daring in advance of her generation, " I sometimes think it would do him a world
of good if he took an occasional spree and sang in
a peat-hag himself! "

" Wheesht, Meg!   Wheesht! " exclaimed Bob, rather alarmed at this outspokenness.   " It won't do to *say* that anyway.   But I'll try to finish early the night and then I'll go down to the manse and face the music."

That evening Bob, with Risp at his heel, set off on his joyless errand with a heavy heart, but with such long swinging strides that he covered the four miles in under an hour.   The minister had been expecting him one of these evenings, and when, through the study window, he saw the shepherd walk up the garden path he assumed his most relentless, uncharitable expression, for—according to his lights—he had a duty to perform.

Bob was ushered into the study, cap in hand— Risp had been ordered to lie at the outer door— and the two men looked each other straight in the eyes.   The minister's hands were under his coat-tails and he did not offer to shake hands—that would have been a weak start which would make his duty all the more difficult.

" Good evening, Mr MacLeod," began Bob, going straight to the point, " I have come down to ask when will it be convenient for you to baptise our little boy."

" I'm sorry, Bob," said the minister in a stern voice, " but I am afraid I cannot baptise your child."

Bob's heart seemed to drop a foot inside his body but he still looked straight at the minister and asked " And why not, sir? "

" Why not! " repeated Mr MacLeod with rising wrath. " Need you ask why not? You should know, Mr Cairns, that baptism is a sacrament that is not to be lightly administered. A father of a family has responsibilities, and in my parish no baptism will be administered to the children of drunkards; and you cannot deny that were shamefully drunk in my presence less than a year ago. I admit that your conduct has been good since then, but the Muir-of-Ord Market will be next week and you know what that means for you! " Then in kindlier tones he continued, " But I'll tell you what I'll do; if you come home sober from the Market I'll baptise your child."

Bob's face flushed. He knew well that he did not neglect his responsibilities as a father, and that he was no drunkard. The condition imposed by the minister was cruel; but the choice before the shepherd was critical, for in those days an unbaptised child was in a precarious position *in* this world, and *for* the next. Bob considered a few moments, and then spoke in his usual quiet way. " I do not admit, Mr MacLeod, that I am a drunkard or that I forget my duties as a father; but I see your point of view and I will do my best to come home sober from the Market." The minister and the shepherd shook hands in silence, and Bob and Risp set off for home.

" How did you get with His Reverence," inquired his wife as she met him at the door.

" Oh, right enough," replied Bob vaguely.

"Good," said Meg, "And when is the bairn going to be baptised?"

"Oh! some day after the Market," evaded Bob. "We didn't just fix an exact day," and he did not disclose anything further.

Market day duly arrived and Bob and Risp were there with the ewes; so were Davie Scott and Jock Elliot and half a dozen other boon companions. The drinking started as soon as the main responsibilities of the day were over, but to the amazement of the others Bob would not join in. At first they were incredulous and regarded his refusal as a great joke. But soon it became quite clear that Bob was taking no drink that day; and he looked very miserable—and no doubt felt even more miserable than he looked. Davie Scott was really perturbed about it; he left his companions and came over to Bob who had just delivered his last lot of ewes to the buyer.

"Bob," said Davie, in that solemn sympathetic way of a friend who is half-drunk, "Bob! for God's sake, what's the matter with you?" and then in an anxious whisper, "You haven't got the cancer?"

"I'm all right, Davie," replied Bob, "but I'm no' drinking any the day." But how he longed to join them! Only he knew the full misery of that day. Davie went back to the crowd, sorely perplexed, and informed them that he couldn't make anything of Bob. "It's just fair puzzling,"

he mourned; and, no doubt with the idea of
getting some light on the mystery, they all took
several more drams.

By four o'clock Bob was ready to start off on
the fifteen mile road for home. But where was
Risp? He couldn't just remember when it was
he had last noticed the dog. But there never had
been any occasion for Bob to look after Risp on
the Market. Indeed it was the other way about!
For, the higher Bob attained to heights of earthly
bliss and freedom from the world's cares, the more
closely did the faithful dog stand by. Bob gave
the special two-toned finger-whistle that Risp knew
so well, but no Risp appeared.

"Risp saw you were sober," said Davie very
solemnly, "and he'll be off on a dander of his
own." Davie's remark brought the only smile of
that dreary day to Bob's lips, for the ironical
thought had flitted through his own mind that
Risp, seeing his master sober, must have concluded
that there was no need for his watchful care and
had gone on some intriguing canine adventure of
his own! For a moment the hurting thought
came to him that Risp might have been stolen by
some scoundrel who had admired the dog's work
and that he might never see his dog again—such
things had happened before—but he thrust that
aside and comforted himself with the reflection
that Risp would turn up all right—indeed the
dog might be home in front of him and give him
a welcome on arrival.

Anyhow, there was no help for it, and Bob, sober, and with a sorry heart, set off on his journey.

When he came to the path that led to the foot-bridge which crossed the burn near his house he stopped, put his first and third fingers in his mouth and whistled in the way that never failed to bring Risp to his side if he were within hearing. No Risp appeared. Bob whistled once again. This time his wife appeared at the door and came towards the bridge.

" Is that you home already, Bob? " she asked inwardly amazed, but casual without.

" Yes, I'm home early," said Bob. And then Meg inquired, " But where is Risp? "

" He is not in the house, then? " countered Bob. " No! he is not here," Meg assured him, " but when did you miss him? "

" I couldn't find him when I was ready to leave the Market," explained Bob, " I was hoping he might be home in front of me, but no doubt he'll turn up soon."

But next day there was no sign of Risp and there was a heart-breaking scene with wee Bobbie when he learned that his playmate had not come home. The father tried to assure him that Risp would be to-morrow, but indeed his own heart was heavy too, for well he knew that if Risp were a free agent he would have been home that day.

Two days later wee Johnnie Cairns was duly baptised.

Day after day and week after week went by and ultimately all hope of his ever returning was given up. Bob missed his faithful assistant on the hill tremendously. The superannuated Glen—to his intense joy and subsequent pain, for he was stiff and old—was invited to accompany his master at his work; but soon another dog had to be trained, for the work was very trying.

Bob's next yearly Market came round and he was there with his new dog. There was no ecclesiastical restraint on the shepherd this time, and Davie Scott and all the rest of them were there, and delighted to see that Bob was himself again. The old crowd were talking at the refreshment tent door when suddenly Bob bit his clay pipe so hard that the stem broke and the head fell to the ground. He was staring at a dog which was "weaving" sweetly at the far side of a lot of sheep. The dog was being directed by a big, florid-faced drover from somewhere in the far south.

"What on earth are you staring at, Bob?" asked Jock Elliot.

"Wait a minute," said Bob. And then as the dog started to run again in response to a command from the drover, Bob whistled. The dog "clapped" as if shot, and then raised his head and looked eagerly around. The drover yelled some other command at him which the puzzled dog proceeded to obey. Bob whistled again! Down went the dog, and again that questioning look! This second interference with his dog was so marked that the drover came over to the group at the tent door, his red face redder with anger. " Who is interfering with my dog? " he demanded. Bob stepped out. " I interfered," he said, very quietly, " that dog is mine."

The language that followed is not to be printed in any respectable book, and the threats . . . . ! But Bob's friends rallied round him and it was not going to be a one-sided affair. Two policemen were called and the cause of the dispute explained to them. The officers of the law were rather perplexed, but Bob, who seldom lost his head or his temper came to their assistance. " That dog is mine," said he, pointing to the dog who was still on the far side of the lot of sheep. " I lost him, or he was stolen from me on this Market last year. This man (pointing to the drover), claims him, and for all I know he may have come by him honestly; but the dog is mine as I will prove to you. If you," continued Bob, turning to the drover, " will walk round to the dog and stand beside him I will whistle and call him by the name of ' Risp,' and if the dog starts to come to me you can call him back, but I can call again, and if the dog leaves you and comes to me that should prove that I am telling the truth when I say the dog is mine."

All but the drover were agreed that that was a fair and even generous line for Bob to take, but the drover realised that he could not afford to refuse the test. He walked over to the dog and spoke kindly to him. Then Bob whistled. The dog sprang to his feet and gazed. Then Bob called "Risp." The dog started to move in the direction of the group at the tent; the drover spoke commandingly to him. "Risp," called Bob again, and this time there was no hesitation. Risp—for Risp it was—came tearing round in the direction of the voice he would never forget, and when he scented and saw his beloved master his expressions of joy were simply indecorous for so staid a gentleman.

The proof of ownership was overwhelming, but Bob, ever considerate of others, suggested to the now dogless drover that he (Bob) and Risp would drive the sheep for a couple of miles down the road where they were to join up with a bigger lot in charge of other shepherds and dogs. The drover gladly accepted and there was no happier dog on the Muir-of-Ord Market that day than our friend Risp as he " kepped " and " clapped " and " checked " at a word from the master he adored.

The gathering at the refreshment tent that evening is historic; Risp had a well-remembered duty to perform, and the light of canine love beamed from his eyes.

K

CHAPTER XXVII

The Charmed Thread or *Snàth Sgochadh Fèithe.*

" MAN, its fine to see them all again, Sandy! "
said the Right Honourable Hector MacLean,
statesman and banking-magnate of the Far East, as
he sat with his brother Sandy on the rustic seat
under the gean tree in the old home garden at
Strathulladale and looked across the valley and
over to the hundred hills whose tops mingled with
the clouds in the far distance—" *Cnoc-na-h-eaglais!*
—*Beinn a'Bhàthaichard!—Sgurr a'Mhuilinn!* and
all the rest of them, so cool and yet so warm and
friendly. God, how often in the scorching sun
out yonder did I think of them! I sometimes
dreamed of them too!—and now after thirty years
—"Here, with true Celtic instinct the speaker
helped himself to a dram to hide his emotion.

" Yes, I suppose they are fine, and very likely I
would miss them too if I didn't see them every
day," replied Sandy who was the one of the family
who had " to stand by the old folks " in the croft
while the rest, one by one went out into the world;
and to make believe that he hadn't noticed his
brother's emotion Sandy poured himself out a
dram too.

In spite of their divergent paths through life the brothers were remarkably alike, for though Hector's hands looked soft beside Sandy's gnarled fists and the London suit was somewhat better cut than the home-spun, the strong massive features were the same, and the clear grey eyes were ridiculously alike—as were the generous mouths that flickered into humour so readily at the corners.

"Aye," continued Hector, "the hills at least have not changed, although, I suppose, nearly everything else is different. There won't be any of the old folks left, and the old customs and superstitions will have died with them."

"Indeed there's not many of the old folks of your day left," agreed Sandy, "and some of the old beliefs have died too. But I'm not so sure that what we used to regard as the superstitions of the older generation may not have a natural enough explanation after all."

"But surely, Sandy," objected the banker, "nobody believes nowadays in *buidseachd* (witchcraft) and the evil eye, and cures like *bùrn-airgid* (silver water), and all that sort of nonsense!"

"Well, anyhow," argued Sandy, "I try to keep an open mind on these things. What would you have said thirty years ago if someone had told you that in a few years' time I could hear you speaking in India as well as I hear you now speaking in that seat? And look at Conan Doyle and Stead and Oliver Lodge? You can hardly call these men cranks or think that they would want to make fools of the rest of us, eh? No, no. I'm thinking that after all there may be more things on this earth than are dreamt of in our philosophy." Sandy was now on a favourite topic and proceeded to enlarge on it.

"Poor Sandy," thought Hector—but he did not say it—"You are as old-fashioned as ever"— "Hullo," he broke in, "who is the budding piper?"

Sandy stopped to listed

"That will be *Seorus Caol's* boy, Calum," he said. "He is daft for the pipes and is always whistling like that and practising the notes."

The whistler was not yet in sight but the notes of "The Atholl Highlanders" came to the ears of the listeners with a lilt and a swing that only one with martial music in his soul could impart. Then the lad came into view at the end of the garden hedge, stepping grandly to the twirling music of his lips and tongue, while at each step the mud of the soft path squeezed up between the toes of his bare feet. On seeing the two men Calum brought strut and tune to a sudden stop and pretended he had only been whistling to his collie.

"Good evening, Calum," Sandy greeted him, "man, you can fairly get the dirls into that one." Calum blushed. "And how are they all with you at home?"

"Fine, thank you," replied Calum, "but the red heifer is lame and I'm just going east to get a *snàth-sgochadh-fèithe* from *Iain Dearg's* wife."

"*Dhia gleidh mi!*" exclaimed Hector, turning to his brother, "Is Iain Dearg's wife still alive and does she still make the *snàth sgochadh fèithe?*"

"That she is and that she does," replied Sandy. Then he politely introduced his brother to the boy. "This is my brother Hector from India, Calum."

They shook hands, Calum remarking shyly, "I have often heard about you."

"Well, here I am in the flesh," said the banker kindly, "and mayby some day you will be going out to India or Australia yourself, Calum; they could do with your kind out there. But what happened to the red heifer?"

"Indeed, I'm not sure," said Calum, "My father thinks it was the black cow that pushed her down the river-bank, but my mother says she is sure it was the *ban'-cheard* (tinker wife) with her evil eye."

"But I thought your people were quite friendly with the tinkers?" said Sandy.

"And so we were till the other day when my father took a rise out of old Kirsty," explained Calum. "When father was raking the stubble field Kirsty came along and begged for a windling of rakings. 'There's the rank and rake a windling for yourself,' said he; Kirsty was very insulted at being asked to work like that. She refused and went away cursing like anything. Father was delighted with the joke, but this morning when my mother was going to milk the cows she is sure she saw Kirsty disappearing in the broom bushes and when mother got to the byre there was the door off the sneck and the red heifer very excited and quite lame on her near hind leg."

"But the *snàth* is only good for accidents," said Hector, the lore of his youth coming back to him. "If it's the evil eye that did it, it's to the wood you should be going for a bit of walnut or elm to carry in the pocket."

"Yes, I know; but I did that to-day already," explained Calum, "and my mother has the bit elm in her pocket now; but father is not satisfied and that is why I am going for a thread from Iain Dearg's wife."

"It's many a day since I got my first *snàth* from her," said Hector reminiscently. "It was for that," extending his left wrist—"and I mind fine how soothed I felt when the thread was tied loosely round it! Calum," he asked, "will you let me do your message for you? Sandy tells me that *Peggi Ruadh's* daughter is now in the shoppie at the bridge and that she sells grand chocolates instead of the ' caravies ' and conversation ' lozengers ' we used to get from her mother. You run down and get some chocolates and I'll go over to Iain Dearg's for the thread."

The boy demurred at taking the proferred money, but it was pressed tactfully, and *Mairi Peggi Ruadh's* chocolates were tempting—and so he agreed. "But you will not be long in coming back?" he stipulated with a sense of responsibility, and the banker assured him he would start off immediately.

In a matter of twenty minutes he was approaching Iain Dearg's house. The old woman stood in the door shading her eyes from the sun and scanning the stranger keenly. Soon she recognised him and stepped slowly out to give him greeting. But it was no old country woman giving humble greeting to one of the great ones of the earth. It was a queenly old lady giving welcome and a blessing to the boy Hector on his return to the home of his fathers; nor did Hector ever dream that it should be otherwise. Both fell into the Gaelic tongue as naturally as flowers expand in the sun, and the past thirty years were as nothing to the banker who was a boy again; and indeed the delusion was not difficult, for the years had left scarce a trace of their passing on this mysterious, kindly woman. The long black frock, the white apron and frilled mutch were just the same and the dark eyes that scorned artificial aid were keen and all-comprehending as ever. Only the hearing was somewhat dulled, Hector noticed.

For a few minutes there was kindly talk of old friends and memories, but soon Hector had to explain the particular urgency of his errand. It seemed quite natural too that this boy should ask Iain Dearg's wife for a *snàth* for the leg of Seorus Caol's red heifer.

"Indeed and that I will," the wife assured him, "it is our duty to help a neighbour if we can";

and straightway she went to an old wicker work-basket from which she selected a pirn of white linen thread. She unwound and broke off about a yard of the thread; this she doubled, and, holding the doubled end between the thumb and forefinger of her left hand she laid the thread on her right knee with the single ends hanging down. Then she spat on the palm of her right hand and with it "rolled" the double thread on her knee. This had the effect of "twining" the threads for an inch or two of their length, and there a knot was tied; then another spit, another "twine" and another knot, and the process was repeated until the thread was all twined, and it had about a dozen knots on the length of it. But all the time that the thread had been manipulated Iain Dearg's wife half muttered, half chanted a *duan* (rhyme). Many a time had suppliant boys and girls tried to catch the words of that *duan*, but the old woman took good care they did not hear much. Now, however, her deafness deceived her, and Hector heard almost every word of it. Freely translated it ran something like this: —

Powers from East and Powers from West,
Powers Above and Powers Below,
Listen to my heart's request;
Join in one and favour show,

> To those buffeted by Scathe,
> In their flesh or bones or blood
> Give calm courage, give strong faith
> To resist Fate's swiftest flood.

And then there followed a third verse which must not be quoted here.

As the words were chanted earnestly again and again the listener became embarrassed, for well he knew that the *duan* should not be " stolen " like this: that the secret could only be imparted voluntarily by a woman to a man or *vice versa*.

" *'Bhean Iain Deirg*," he said apologetically, " I am sorry, but I could not help hearing the words of the *duan*."

For a moment she flushed with vexation. Then she smiled resignedly. " Well, well, Hector; maybe it's the hand of Providence. I am now an old woman and it's high time I was handing on the secret. You were always a clever, understanding lad, and I have no son living of my own; now listen and be sure you get it right. I got it from my grandfather, *Alastair a'Bhreabadair* (Sandy the Weaver), fifty-two years ago when I was only forty years of age and if it has not always done good, it has often helped, and it never did any harm."

And so it was that Iain Dearg's wife, the granddaughter of *Alastair a'Bhreabadair* handed down to the Right Honourable Hector MacLean the secret of the *snàth-sgochadh Fèithe* at the same time as she handed him the last *snàth* she would ever make; for once disclosed, the "gift" was hers no longer.

CHAPTER XXVIII

Memories or *An Gleann 'San Robh Mi Og.*

ONCE every year, for a few fleeting days, I return to the place of my birth—*an gleann's an robh mi og*. Just why, it would be hard to explain. For the chairs by the old fire-side have now new tenants; the dear old friends who filled them are gone. It is the same throughout the glen, too. One by one the old folks have been gathered to their fathers. A new brood has arisen that to me is alien. Only an old school-comrade here and there. But to meet these—to look into their eyes again—to feel the firm hand-grip—to hear the warmth in their voices, is one of the deepest joys in life. As we move about the world we are ever forming new friendships. But new friends can never be quite like these. We see new friends as through a glass, darkly, but into and through the friends of our childhood days we see with eyes of utter understanding.

So that the annual sojourn in the glen brings a mixture of emotions. Frankly, the holiday never comes quite up to anticipations. But the anticipation itself is grand!—and so is the retrospect.

Weeks before the great day, thoughts of it intrude themselves and give a lightsome lift to the daily darg. The process accumulates as the day approaches. Plans are discussed; programmes mapped out for filling in the rosy hours. Quite likely most of the plans will never materialise. But look at the joy of making them!

Then on the day itself there is the bustle of getting to the station and scrambling for seats in the train. By the time we recover our breath we are well away from the smoke, and the sordid surroundings of the city, and racing up the great north road. Past Blair Atholl we climb into the heather. And now, with every mile there is a subtle change. It is as if a weight on your chest had been removed. You can fill your lungs with the honey-scented air of the hills. You are like a horse trotting homewards. Not an old horse either, but a young high-stepper with ears aprick. And when you reach the *druim* (ridge) between Carr-bridge and Culloden that affords you the first distant view of the hills and Bens of Ross. . . . ! Confound those splashes! I had to use my hankie —and the bairns wondered if Dad were catching a cold. . . .

One evening last autumn, I indulged in sadly pleasant retrospect—the sort of emotional ecstasy one sometimes achieves on a visit to the old church-yard. But this was not in the church-yard. I walked along the braes, and in less than a mile, I passed where nine houses had been—the homes of people I remember—but of which now only ruins, or less, remain.

Beside that rowan tree there stood old Ciorsti's cottage. Not one trace is left; there is a rabbit burrow just about the spot where the old lady used to sit and spin.

Beneath those lumpy mounds covered with green grass are the stones that used to form the walls of Rory the shoemaker's workshop. It would be just here by the ingle neuk where Rory used to sit on a backless oak chair cutting out the uppers for the eight shoemakers that sat in two rows down the room, each intent on turning out an article that would be a masterpiece. As I gazed at the spot it seemed to me that Rory was there again. I seemed to see him straighten his back as he used to do, and inhale a copious *snaoisean* (snuff) from yon queer old *scrogag* he had.

Not even the *larach* (site) of the old *breabadair's* house is left, where in other days the shuttle flew swiftly this way and that to build the homely web.

Twice this autumn did I climb to the top of the Ben. She is the only thing that is changeless; even her mists are the same. On the way to the Fuaran Mor we startled coveys of grouse. There was a water-ouzel fishing in the pool at the Falls and we saw the brown trout like dark shadows flitting in the pools of the burn; while on its banks we had a rare feast of *Oighreagan* (cloud berries).

The mountain was in frowning mood both days. From the Big Well to the summit there was a rolling mist that made the sheep as big as deer and the hares as big as sheep. The few ptarmagans we saw, too, were magnified to the size of geese. Not one blink of distant view did the fickle jade vouchsafe. But once—just a matter of moments—there was a rift in the rolling canopy, and (like part of a film projected on a gigantic screen) we got a perfect view of the Corrie with the sun blazing down from above and a herd of deer streaking up the Eastern slope.